Wretch

Haunted by Shadows — Rescued by Jesus

SEAN WHEELER

Wretch
Haunted by Shadows - Rescued by Jesus
by Sean Wheeler

Printed in the United States of America.

ISBN 9781498486736

Editing provided by Rudy Rodriguez, the author of *Before There Was*, a fictional account of the universe before Genesis, available at Amazon.com. Editing also provided by Pastor Ben Salgado, Resurrection Fellowship Church, Loveland, Colorado.

Final Edits provided by: www.FirstEditing.com (Editor: Virginia)

www.xulonpress.com

ABOUT THE AUTHOR

Wretch: *Haunted by Shadows, Rescued by Jesus* focuses on Sean Wheeler's story of healing from sexual and physical abuse he experienced as a young boy. In a series of personal essays, Sean explores the depression, low self-esteem, negative thoughts, and self-destructive actions that stem from his abuse. He discusses the real life effects of sexual abuse, such as trouble maintaining relationships and jobs.

Depending on his faith in God and God's love for him, he began finding answers to his questions such as "Why did this happen?" and "Why would God let this happen to me?" In a raw and emotional description of what the long road to recovery looks like, Sean writes about his experiences, from the obstacles to finding the right kind of support center, to visiting a therapist, to confronting his memories. Writing from the perspective of a man in a situation that often stigmatizes men and boys for wanting help, he aims to help other men find the courage and strength to look for their own healing.

Sean attends Resurrection Fellowship Church in Loveland, Colorado. Jonathan Wiggins, Senior Pastor.

CONTENTS

Dedication ix

Chapter ONE: Why This Book Is Different 11
    – I Was Not Strong Enough Alone
    – Help for Christian Guys
    – Why Did God Let This Happen?
    – False Starts, Failed Efforts
    – What Will "They" Think of Me?
    – It Gets Better
Chapter TWO: No Words, No Voice, No Self 24
    My Journal
Chapter THREE: I Am Haunted by Shadows. 31
Chapter FOUR: My Path to Darkness 41
Chapter FIVE: A Target Is Formed. 46
    – Scrambled Signals
    – The Good Old Days
    – Little Wimp
    – Fishing Trips
    Author's Note
Chapter SIX: Invisible Boy, Voice Restored. 68
    – Finding Invisible Chains
    – Never Tell
Chapter SEVEN: No Safe Place. 78
    – Look Me in the Eyes

Chapter EIGHT: Redeemed 83
  – First Steps to Healing
  – The Holy Spirit's Hand
  – The Defeat of Shame, Guilt, and Fear
Chapter NINE: The Anger Box: A Turning Point. 93
Chapter TEN: Finding Anger 97
  – Open the Door
  – A Light in the Darkness
Chapter ELEVEN: You Have to Go Now! 108
Chapter TWELVE: Spiritual Warfare, Intensified 119
  – But Deliver Us from Evil
Chapter THIRTEEN: The Battle Begins. 127
  – Twelve Shadows, Twelve Faces of Evil
  – Freedom Found
Chapter FOURTEEN: Hear the Frogs Singing! 139
Chapter FIFTEEN: What Now, Lord? 143
  – A New Mission
  – God Only Knows
  – A Safe Challenge
Chapter SIXTEEN: 6:33 & Thunder on the Mountain. 159
  – A New Counselor
  – Moving Forward
  – A New Season
  – A New Understanding
Chapter SEVENTEEN: Conversations with the Spirit. 169
  – Rebuilding an Old Friendship
  – No Fear: Tell Them
Chapter EIGHTEEN: My Soul to Keep! 177
  – Thank You Notes from the Fire
  – A Prayer for Us

DEDICATION

To my wife Susan, whose quiet grace gently started me down this road to healing. I love you more than I can ever begin to describe in words. You are God's blessing in my life, a gift to my soul.

To my family who know my story now and support me. I love you all.

To my Christian family, who helped me get through this and find my way toward the light and love of God. There are hundreds of you, too many to name. I will be forever grateful.

To Alex, my friend and fellow survivor online, who endured a life of pure hell on earth yet you encouraged me and gave me hope and friendship. We have never met, but you will always be my brother in this fight.

Most of all, I give thanks to God, who never gave up on me, even when I had given up on myself. Thank you, Jesus!

You shall know the truth and the
truth shall set you free.
Jesus
John 8:32

For our struggle is not against flesh and blood,
but against the rulers, against the authorities,
against the powers of this dark world,
and against the spiritual forces of evil
in the heavenly realms.
Ephesians 6:12

Chapter ONE

I love the Lord for He heard my voice, He heard my cry for mercy. Because He turned his ear to me, I will call on Him as long as I live.

Psalm 116: 1–2

WHY THIS BOOK IS DIFFERENT

The pages of this book are lifted from my past, but also taken from my life in freedom today, with me having found hope and a purpose. What I lived through in the past does not define me anymore; it is not the end of my journey, and it does not have to be the end of yours either. What you will find here is painful to read in some places, but keep in mind, this ends really well. My story is not a sad one; it is one of victory.

This is also not a novel and it doesn't flow like one. Each chapter could be an essay in itself. They follow a timeline of my journey from fear to freedom as it happened in my life. This chapter tells why this book is unlike others on abuse recovery. Few books are written from a male perspective, and fewer still focus on being rescued by God. Chapter two talks about how I found the strength to start counseling. Most survivors will likely tell you that finding a counselor is a very hard step to take because of trust issues. Chapters three through thirteen are taken from a journal I wrote during counseling. They follow the steps we worked through in that process. Chapters fourteen through seventeen describe my continued journey in healing after being baptized by the Holy Spirt, and how that one event changed my life forever in 2011. The last chapter holds a few things I could not place anywhere else. It's about a journey in healing that continues in me, and such journeys often take wandering paths.

I wrote it for other guys who lived through abuse, for those currently living in abusive situations, and for those who love them enough to try to help them find freedom and healing. In this chapter, I'll describe a few of the painful questions survivors may have, ones that I had in the start of my rescue and healing process, and it outlines the answers that brought me to where I am today. Today, I am free. It was not easy at all, but it was very much worth the effort. As I started walking through my process of facing the abuse, I found out that there are very few resources of support available for guys, especially when it comes to the problem of sexual abuse. There are fewer still for Christian men and boys as most of the books available are not written from a faith perspective.

I have to be clear. This book is *not* a replacement for counseling, but it shows you how I found the courage to approach a counselor and to hang on throughout that process. Healing really is possible, and I am living proof of that. So that's me, a guy who survived and who found a home and freedom in Christ. A guy who wants now to tell others that there is a place for you to find the same freedom from that pain too.

– I Was Not Strong Enough Alone –

This is also not just another story about someone who was abused and one day magically decided to simply forget that it ever happened. I've had people tell me that it's time to "just let it all go" as if letting it go was something easy to do. They do not understand that I tried to do that, many times, and failed at it just as many times. It's not easy, and for the record, there is absolutely nothing especially different about me either. At least not the "me" who tried to fix this on my own. God says in Him we are all a masterpiece, and that is where I found strength to do this. I was not always willing to go along, and in fact I pretty much had to be dragged into the process by the Holy Spirit. Today, I am so glad He did that for me.

Before the Spirit pulled me up, I had just accepted that "it" was part of me and there was no way I could change how that made me feel inside. I pretty much figured that what happened was my fault, that I deserved it, and that I should be glad I didn't get worse. I did not trust the world and believed there was no safe place for me anywhere if people really knew about my past. Simply put, I had given up on myself, and written myself off as having little to offer. In my mind, that was it, the end of my story. Had you cornered me not that many years ago and asked who I am, you might have gotten this for an answer:

"I am the leftover shell of some kid used up years ago, nothing more."

What a pack of lies.

Funny thing though, God refused to accept any of that from me, and it was through Him that I finally found healing. Today, I'll give you a completely different answer. Today, I will tell you that I am a masterpiece. I am a child of God and I was never, *ever* defined by what people did to me or said to me. I am defined by the Creator of the Universe alone, who calls me His own. He has the same answer for you, too.

Healing and taking those first steps is not easy. It would take me down a bumpy road that I did not always understand, but I went from being broken to survivor and now I'm a thriver. I discovered too that the only thing holding me back was a belief in things that were simply lies, all of them, lies of the enemy. But the loving hand of Christ can break those chains.

– Help for Christian Guys –

For the record, I am not the source of help; I'm just the messenger. The source is the Spirit of God, and He really is reaching out to you. I had tried a lot of secular approaches, and nothing worked. The reality is that male survivors sometimes face hostility when we try to find help from the wreckage of abuse. We get hostility from other men who think we're weak, or hostility from some women with an agenda that coldly insists "ladies first." I've even heard people say that males cannot be sexually abused because, after all, they like it. (Yes, I've been told that one too.)

It's as if some people fear that any attention focused on males will turn the focus away from the problem of abuse against girls and women, as if one is real and the other only imagined. I have talked to guys who went into rape crisis centers and were driven out because their "male presence" alone made people there uncomfortable, although boys and some men have been attacked by males, too. Some were hurt by women as well. Sadly, in some places, those two facts do not matter. Just walk in the circles of survivors and you'll find out that a negative reception for guys in support centers is more common than you might think, and that is just wrong.

I have never met another male survivor who wanted to take support away from women. Not one. However, as I found out, no one can deal with this very well on their own so there is a need for resources available to men and boys. I would add, too, that shining a light on the problem of abuse of guys does not diminish one bit the light shining on the problems women face. Nothing could be further from the truth, and the fact is that men (and boys) *are* abused too, so the world can just deal with it. If that idea makes some people uncomfortable, it's their problem and not ours. Guys should not be treated differently simply because of their gender. We have different stories than women and girls, but we have shared hurts with them. That is what should matter. Ignoring this doesn't make it go away, and there is strength in numbers.

For me, the secular approaches didn't help at all and I had tried a number of them over the years. I am not saying they are necessarily bad, just saying they did nothing for me. What helped me? Building a relationship with God. When it comes to healing, I found out that He is the great healer. For some people that idea sounds old-fashioned or quaint and outdated, or maybe they are embarrassed or even offended by the thought of asking God for help. God lets people decide on their own if He is to be a part of their life or not. It's called free will.

I chose Him because I had ended up with having no other place to turn. I was not even sure it would work. Not because I didn't believe in God, but because, deep down in my soul, the one I did not believe in was myself. So nothing ventured, nothing gained, as the saying goes. What did I gain? Mercy, healing, and strength is what. That freedom God offers is huge and there's enough to go around for all who seek it. I encourage you to take that step and let the Creator work in and heal you as He has done in me.

To God, the abuse of *any* child is a big deal, girl or boy. It is time the world stopped treating boys (and men) differently, and it is time the world stopped insisting that the only acceptable choices are those that leave out God as an option for healing.

– Why Did God Let This Happen? –

Truth be told, many books about recovery from abuse don't include God in the process. For some reason, in today's secular world, He's just not considered necessary anymore. After all, God "let" this happen so He must *not* care is the reasoning, but that's not at all true. Some books even claim that a faith-based approach to healing can do more harm than good if a person was hurt by a pastor or someone else from church. My answer to that comment is simple.

Jesus got hurt by church people too.

Regardless of what anyone says, God is not the building or even the worshipers. God is God, and yes some very flawed people claim to follow Him. None of that changes a thing about who God is, or His love for us, or His ability to set you free. Before turning to Him, I had tried a lot of things yet the past kept coming back in nightmares and flashbacks. I felt stuck in mud so deep that I could not escape from its depths. Without God, I did not have the keys to really under-standing what happened to me or to know where the blame actually falls. Now I do.

So yes, abuse happens in churches. It also happens in schools, parks, shopping malls, in the woods, in barns, in attics, and it happens in private homes. Yet today, there is no attack on any other institution like the one being waged against God or His church. Make no mistake, the enemy (satan) is behind all of it, and he does not want you to be free. The enemy loves abuse and how abusers carry out their plans. It happens in the shadows, where the enemy operates, and it happens in probably every town worldwide. It happens to *one in six* boys, according to an organization called 1in6, which supports male abuse survivors. They have a list of studies from the last twenty years to support that statistic. My counselor told me the same thing to show me I'm not alone is this. That is how big the problem is. Yet the world is often just silent on the issue. If you went through it, you would know how isolated guys can feel. I will not be isolated or silent anymore. My testimony here addresses the abuse of one boy and the rescue of one man, me, who found healing through the love of Christ.

In this book, I will tell you the answers I found to some tough questions others now ask me as a Christian survivor, such as: *Why did God just stand there and let this happen?* Here is my response today, and scripture supports it: We live in a world of free will, and Christians are not free from the free will of others. Sadly, that is even true for children. It is why I believe God *commands* that adults protect them, and His judgment is pretty severe for those who seek to harm them. God didn't just stand there and turn His back, and today, I know He did save me from death in the moment and in my future too. God did rescue me!

In fact, as I learned at church, God's judgment is a lot more severe than anything we could think up, so we need to leave justice in His hands because God will hold people accountable. You can be absolutely certain of that fact. Once I accepted that idea, there was a whole lot of anger inside that dissolved. I don't have to worry about them anymore. Also know this, scripture promises that God will take what was meant for our harm and turn it to our good and to His glory! *(See Genesis 50:20. "You intended to harm me, but God intended it for good to accomplish what is now being done, the saving of many lives.")*

– False Starts, Failed Efforts –

If you have read this far, you are either a survivor or you know someone who is struggling through this. I would bet that like me, they would say, *"I've had too many false starts and failed efforts before, so why try again, why now?"*

Why did all of my other past efforts fail? The answer is because God was not in the game. The enemy was sure on the field and playing hard to keep me down. He tried to stop me from moving forward as often as he could. This time, the enemy's plans failed. God wanted me to be free, and all the forces of darkness cannot stop what God has ordained will come to pass.

Once God came into the picture, I started down a road leading to freedom from the past. Healing did not happen for me in an instant. I am a work in progress with some difficult things I still need to face, but I am far better on the inside now than ever before. Whatever is left, I won't face it alone. I can stand against any struggle the enemy throws up at me such as flashbacks, triggers, etc. Those things cannot defeat me anymore, as there is a new source of strength in me that won't let them.

– What Will "They" Think of Me? –

We should not have to choose between living in hurt and how our past makes *others* feel. Does it really matter what they think, whoever "they" are? It shouldn't, but the tragic truth is that many victims of abuse are afraid to deal with it simply because of people might and react. No one should have to stay stuck in misery because others may not know how to handle this. It's really their problem and not ours, yet children and adult survivors are supposed to handle it somehow without support. That idea is simply wrong in so many ways, yet guys are very susceptible to this trick from the enemy. I was solidly there, too, in the camp of "real men would think I'm a loser if they found out about this stuff." I discovered that real men who are believers in Christ support me now. They see me as Jesus does, and they don't offer condemnation. The opinions of others who would condemn me just don't matter today.

Real men don't blame the victim, and they don't judge the victim either. We are not losers; in fact, the opposite is true because we survived something pretty horrible as kids, and that takes amazing strength. I have talked to other victims of abuse who would say the same thing. If that is you saying "loser" to yourself, let me ask you this. If you already see yourself as weak, what do you have to lose by trusting Christ? Let Him be your protector and provide your strength. Believe me, He will give you strength you never thought possible. He did it for me.

Taking that step means crossing the chicken line as my pastor would say, because the enemy uses *fear* to keep victims quiet, as I was for far too many years. I will not be quiet ever again. Abusers commit their crimes in secret for the enemy's gain, so I'll do what I can to expose those tactics. They are good at twisting the minds of children to believe lies such as *you* are the one to blame and *you* are the one at fault, and no one will want *you* if they know what *you* have done. All of those "you" statements leave a mark, especially in the mind of a child. I believed those lies for years. I was caught in a trap that I did not even know existed, which was set for me by the enemy. Now, today, in this light of knowing whose I am, those lies hold no power over me anymore. None! It does not matter now what others say about me, only what God says about me. God does not care where any of us have *been,* He only cares about where we are going.

For me, the sexual abuse started around the time I was five or six years of age. To this day, I don't know the exact number of times I was molested, and I don't care now because it does not matter. What matters is abuse set my early life on a difficult path into adolescence and adulthood, and I really did not trust anyone easily or well. There are millions around the world like me, millions who have similar stories and a shared pain, who live in silence. We are usually invisible to the world around us, because fear turns us into masters of disguise. I had fear pounded into me after events sometimes. They hit me or scared me with harsh, angry words or made threats against things I cared about, like our dog. It worked on a five-year-old.

Abusers use fear to keep people, especially children, from getting help. Here is my answer to it today. My testimony is not a sad story. It is one of victory and it has a good ending. Your story can too. God never intended for the actions of others to define any of us. Today, I stand redeemed. How is that possible? It is because God has more than enough love and patience to heal all who seek His help, and to walk them through it.

Fear is not of God, it is from the enemy and it's another lie he tells. My fear of them and their threats is gone. When it does try to creep up on me now, I remember 2 Timothy 1:7:

"For God hath not given us the spirit of fear; but of power, and of love, and of a sound mind."

– It Gets Better –

Yes, it really does get better. You are definitely not invisible and you are certainly not alone. I am still a work in progress in my own healing, but every single person alive has *something* to work on. No one has it all down perfect, and don't believe for a minute that anyone is perfect no matter how much they seem to be so. Where am I now? I am so much further along from where I ever imagined I could be at the start of this. The nightmares have mostly stopped, and they will never be able to trigger me again as they once did. I can deal with them today thanks to God. I have also moved beyond the stages of having to identify and acknowledge that the abuse really happened to a place of acceptance that it did happen. Like many survivors, I used to blame myself, but not anymore. We can move forward in peace through Christ, and for me, every day with Him on this journey just keeps getting better.

We cannot change my past but that doesn't matter to me anymore. The abuse no longer defines who I am. Actually it *never* defined me or anyone else, because God never measures us by what others chose to do to us. Thankfully, He doesn't measure us by our own mistakes either when we turn to Him. Every day is now a learning experience with God. As my pastor told me at the start of this process, my freedom in Christ was instant, but my growth in discovering Him will be a lifelong thing. OK, let's go!

Please consider something if you are thinking this may not be the book for you. The "thing" that we fear is an illusion. It looks very real because bad things *really* did happen to us as children and that is what we remember. Yet the *ideas* about ourselves that we learned from those events are the real illusions. They are painted in lies on a canvas of deception, and were created by evil when it was spoken into our lives as children. The biggest lie of all is that somehow *we* were to blame, we were responsible. A child cannot consent; they can only comply. Because children are innocent and naturally trust, they will simply believe the things adults say and that includes lies. That image of self-blame is a fake, a complete fraud.

Step through it now and you'll see the only thing that is real. That is the freedom promised by Christ. When you push through the lies, the illusion will shatter and be replaced by truth. Maybe not all at once, but it will shatter into nothingness in the end. When that happens, you will know who you really are and that is not what you were taught by evil. Today, I look at that pile of broken shards at my feet and laugh at how phony it all was, but it took work and courage for me to get here. That courage was not of me; it came to me from the Holy Spirit when I agreed to surrender to His leading. He will generously give it to you too.

So this is my story, and much of it comes from a journal I kept of my process in the first difficult months. The rest comes from the incredible places my freedom has taken me since then. I had to write as part of my therapy process. Writing gave me a way to get it out when I first started meeting with a counselor as I just could not say the words out loud about what happened. Now, I'm writing to help others find healing as well.

My journal starts in January 2011, when I was yet several months away from the day that would change my life forever. I'll admit that I've edited some things out, as my writing through tears was sometimes less than clear. Some parts are gone as I just don't need to see them in print anymore, and I really don't have to share everything for my healing either. Every abuse survivor probably has parts of their story they don't want to keep talking about with anyone. If and when I need to, I can talk to God or any one of the many believers in my life now who encourage me, and I can talk to them without fear.

My story is for others who still struggle to get free from the nightmares that so many abuse victims share. For us, it is a common sadness. So it is for other survivors that I write this, and for those who love them enough to want to help. It is for those who feel caught up in an endless cycle of dead-end efforts when they try to find real healing, and for those who are simply tired of being tired.

Who am I now? I am one who has a name and it isn't any of the words and labels that were plastered on me over the years. My name is redeemed. My name is child of the one true King. My name is Sean. This is my testimony. I hope that you will read this and also choose to start a personal relationship with Christ. There are tough lessons ahead, but welcome to the School of Mercy! Take that step, it'll lead to incredible things and a whole new sense of who you are and whose you are, too.

Chapter TWO

"You gain strength, courage and confidence by every experience in which you really stop to look fear in the face. You are able to say to yourself, 'I have lived through this horror. I can take the next thing that comes along.' You must do the thing you think you cannot do."

Eleanor Roosevelt

NO WORDS, NO VOICE, NO SELF

I don't really know much about Eleanor Roosevelt except that she was a strong woman. She was right, too. Amazing things can happen when we *do* the thing we think is impossible for us. For many years, I had told myself that there was no way I could ever do that one thing, which was talk to anyone about "this stuff." That was the impossible obstacle I had placed in my path. It was the wall I would not ever try to climb because my fear of not knowing what was on the other side kept me from trying. That wall did not protect me. It kept me trapped with things I had no way to fix on my own.

Taking that first step came out of sheer desperation to be honest. It felt like I had two choices. Try counseling or die inside. I had reached a desperate milestone in life as I had lost my job, again. Once again the enemy came around, bringing up my past in whispers of things like, *"Serves you right. You were only ever good for one thing, and you're too old for that now. Should have just died after you left high school."*

Of course that was a lie, and the enemy (satan) was behind it. He is the father of all lies, according to scripture. I didn't want to die, but options for me seemed limited, and the whispers seemed to hold some truth in the natural, in what my world had always been. How many times had I lost my job because of things that didn't make sense? Here I was again wondering why; how did I bring this about when I had tried so hard to be the best employee I could be? They even gave me great references. It made no sense, and the whispers continued.

Someone said once that you find your destiny on the road you take to avoid it, and this layoff turned out to be a good thing because it drove me to a seek out a counselor. I had tried that before and it didn't work, but this time I would try a Christian counselor. It was, for me, the only path I had left to take. I would take that step, and it would turn out to be the first of many such steps that were to change my life forever. God was working in me in those days even though I didn't really know it. Today, I have let go of being a victim and become more than just a survivor. I am now a thriver. I am free and also new. I am becoming the one who God intended me to be all along.

How did I push myself into counseling? The first step takes strength, courage and confidence. I found those things lacking in myself, but somewhere deep inside they were there. It would become clear, too that all three build up after taking the first step, and they continue to build with each new step taken. Think of David facing Goliath. Here he was, some scrawny teenager standing up to a man who was huge in physical stature at over seven feet tall, with a fierce reputation to match. In the natural world, seeing a man like Goliath would tell any rational person that this was not a guy to be messed with by a scrawny kid. Yet David did not look at Goliath as a giant because he had his mind fixed on God and not the brute in front of him. David had no fear that I know of from reading scripture. He had the strength of God, and knew what to do without hesitation. It was that simple for him. My sense in reading scripture is that David had no doubt he would take Goliath down with one stone from a sling-shot, because David knew that God was with him on that battlefield.

This would be my battlefield, and the "Goliath" I faced was my past. I was about to meet it head-on in a fight for my life. Like David, God would be with me every step of the way, however, don't get the idea that I had David's confidence as I was going into counseling. I didn't. What I had was enough energy left inside to say OK, I'll try *once* more. Maybe it was growth of a small seed of faith someone had planted in me years ago. Whatever it was I had it, and that was all God needed.

How do you prepare for counseling after deciding to take that step? I suggest two ways. Start with prayer; it was the first thing I did. Even though I was not sure if God cared about my prayers, I had to try it. Prayer does not have to be complicated and full of big words. You can simply say, *Father, help me.*

I did that once, at nine years old, hiding in a closet and crying hard after one event, the last one in my memory, actually. "Events" is what I call those times. I only said those words, "Father help me" and God answered immediately. The tears stopped, and the hurt was gone in that moment. I had no clue sitting there in the dark on that summer day about what had just happened when I said those words, but I remember it clearly. God answered me. Those tears stopped and I even tried making them start again, but it didn't work. The Father had answered a nine-year-old's prayers. Recently, I came to understand the fullness of His answer on that day. This past summer, I realized that not long after my prayer in the closet we moved away from that town, and *they never got to me again*. Now that is an answer to a child's prayer. Thank you, Jesus!

My former pastor, who has now retired, says that may have been the day I was saved. The key thing is I did not use any formal approach dictated by others. I used the words of a child in pain, and God heard me, loud and clear. It was the start of my praying life. It would be a long time from that day to where I am now, but keep in mind that God answers prayers in His time and not ours. God's timing is always perfect even if we don't understand it. Start praying and keep praying, and just know that He really does want to have that conversation with you. You can speak to Him as you would to a friend, because that is who He truly is. Don't worry about finding perfect words, just start talking. He'll listen, and He knows your heart.

The second step was definitely harder because it's all about trust. I had to trust the idea that talking to a counselor would not hurt again, and trust that God would lead me through and out of it. For a lot of survivors, our trust has been so badly violated that it does not come easy to us. It never did for me. I viewed the world as a dangerous place for someone like myself, at least the part of my history that I had kept locked inside. What I'm asking you to do now is trust God. Tell Him that, or that you want to trust Him in this. God will get it if you are not fully there because He knows where you have been. That's it. I know from my own experience that when you start a conversation with Him in prayer, God starts to work in you. Not only that, but scripture also says God *will* finish the work He has started within us. *(See Philippians 1:6 "Being confident of this, that he who began a good work in you will carry it on to completion until the day of Christ Jesus.")* That is a promise He made, and God always keeps His word. I found in taking these two steps that it would be the start of Him bringing that promise to life in me.

I know it's very hard; believe me, I really do. There were times I wanted to give up, too. It took a long time for me to put my foot out for that first step and cross one of many chicken lines to come. I finally did it, because I had grown tired of fighting this on my own. Honestly, I had tried everything else. If this didn't work, I figured that at least I would not be any worse off for the effort. Of course everything I tried before did not include letting God take control of the process. This time, I would do that. It worked all right, and through it, I found my way out of the darkness that had lived inside of me for so many years.

You can do this, but you have to know inside that you are worth it, too. God already knows that, and He knows how hard it is for abuse victims to believe it. After all, we got told so many lies, all of which pointed a finger of blame right at us, lies told by the abusers and the enemy. Kids believe them, which is why they are so evil.

Stand in front of a mirror and look at yourself. Do you really see someone who deserved all of that? No! You did not! Were you to blame? No! Let that message sink in. You may not totally believe it now, but start to try. Let it start to be part of who you say you are today. It is the truth, and it will become part of your new foundation. Say "I am not worthless, and I deserve to be free!" Another part of that new foundation. Ultimately, that foundation is built on a relationship with

Christ and it cannot be shaken or destroyed. Imagine that freedom in you, what it will be like, and set that as your goal.

For me, once it was clear I needed counseling, I made up my mind to try a Christian counselor. I never gave up believing in God. I had simply accepted the false idea that maybe He did not have any use for me. My decision was to try something new, and finding a path in faith was the only choice left for me. Thinking back on it now, it's clear God was leading me in that choice. How that all came about, such as meeting my counselor, I'll talk about later. For now, I'll say this, God led me to a woman who uses what is called a Sozo process. What is that? It is like having a direct face-to-face conversation with the Holy Spirit, and it works.

Sozo is a Greek word. It's translated as meaning you are saved, healed, and delivered. Sozo ministry leads directly to healing and deliverance from the inside. It is not easy, but it lets you *safely* get to the source of things that are keeping you from having a personal connection with the Father, Son and Holy Spirit. It is safe because the Holy Spirit is right there walking with you all the way, and you know it. The Spirit is facing every obstacle with you. Through that, you can become the one God always wanted you to be.

My counselor was able to lead me in this, and you will need help from someone very strong in faith too, but it works. Sozo is something more common in charismatic churches, but it has nothing to do with handling snakes or other weird stuff sometimes associated with the charismatic movement. Do not believe those lies about charismatic Christians or any other believers, either. There are many good people of faith who want to help. God is alive, so pray that He leads you to the right people, the right church, and the right counselor. He answered that cry for help from me.

My Journal

The following chapters started with a journal that I wrote during counseling. This is mostly the way I wrote it down either before or after each session. I've added the chapter titles, etc. and expanded on my journal in places to make things clear, but the raw emotions of each session are still there in my words. God would refine me in the fire through this, and He is still doing that today. Spoiler alert... the Lamb wins!

Chapter THREE

There is sacredness in tears. They are not the mark of weakness but of power. They speak more eloquently than ten thousand tongues. They are messengers of overwhelming grief, of deep contrition, and unspeakable love.

Washington Irving

January 2011

One month into counseling

I AM HAUNTED BY SHADOWS

A nyone who has experienced abuse knows about tears. I have cried gallons of them in lonely days and nights by myself, reliving the sadness in me and never really understanding it or being able to wash it away with my tears. To me, it seemed like no one ever noticed. I'm told that God collects our tears in a bottle and records them in a ledger as a way to show us that He is not only aware of our sadness but also that He will not forget it. I want so much to believe that, to believe something is possible. What is the something I want? I want to be completely done with this and have it out of my life permanently and forever.

Until the day I started counseling, I did not understand Washington Irving's quote above, but I'm starting to. In response to the tears, my counselor told me *"You have to write your story."* I wanted to know why. I have seen evil and looked it in the eyes, and I don't want to see it again. It hurt me badly but she says that for me to really heal, I have to speak in one way or another. Writing is that path for me, and this will be one of the first steps, and it's not going to be fun or easy. OK, I will try, even if it means writing about "the shadows."

I am haunted by shadows. They are real enough and have been a part of my life for as long as I can remember. The shadows keep on a regular, painful, and cruel schedule with me even today. They never want me to forget that I was molested. I can never see their faces, but I cannot remember a time when they weren't in my life in some form.

They hide in my mind and come out at night to walk in my dreams, waiting for when I have to sleep again so they can go to work. They also do not want me to forget their ever-present nature in my life. Over the course of time, they have never identified themselves or shown their full form to me. They are cowards and they are evil. During the day, they hide in the corners of my mind where I cannot see them, but I can still hear their judgmental whispers with every new challenge I face.

"Loser, you'll mess this up too."

I sometimes think on those dreams from the night before and just wonder what it all really means. I hate it, and I hate those images. All that does is distract me from living, or at least trying to live and to fit in or belong somewhere. I don't know who or what they are, but I know that those shadows who haunt me live inside of me. They have been there for decades. Even as a little kid, I always knew they were there, because at night, the shadows would come out and plague my thoughts. They hate me and I am powerless to stop them. I have tried everything I could think of to stop the dreams they pour into my sleep, from prayer to reading self-help articles to talking to the psychologist at college.

None of that ever worked, so here I am, finally talking to a new counselor. She's a powerful Christian and a survivor of abuse, too. There is this light that shines in her. I love that, but it is beyond difficult to do these things she asks of me. I must. I sometimes wonder if she's really an angel in human form because it seems like she has this ability to know why I'm hurting without me having to provide a lot of details for her. Much as I fully hate the idea of looking more closely at all of it, I have to face down the shadows if I am to be really free from them.

God's help is needed, and at this point I know I've got it. I can't count the number of times I've prayed and asked that this all go away or get fixed. It seemed like all I got in return for an "answer" was laughter from the darkness. God has answered those prayers now, and He never laughs at my pain. The shadows still do. I am so tired of them, and I'm praying hard this works just to see God having the last laugh.

Before I can talk about what I clearly remember, I must try to describe the shadows. It feels like so much of what I can see in my memories is shrouded in mists and dark clouds. I have a few totally clear memories of some bad things that happened, more than I would prefer to have, in fact. The shadows flash those snippets of images briefly in my dreams almost nightly. You can't close your eyes in a dream, so I see sad and frightful pictures taken through the lens of my own eyes. The shadows do that so I will never forget the things that happened. Along with the pictures, I get a message:

"Your fault" are the words I hear. *"All your fault, boy! Served you right, too!"*

That's my reality at the start of this. I don't understand those words, but I still believe them. It's been my understanding of this stuff for as long as I can remember. If there is a "why" behind those words, I don't know what it is. Parts of me just don't care anymore, either. I gave up caring years ago. Those pictures are clear enough. They are incomplete, but regardless, I see enough and those memories never change. I'm left to wonder what else happened when I am awake. The shadows enjoy these stabs at my soul with painful snapshots of my past, shards of little mental post-it notes flung at me as reminders of things that were done in dark places.

I guess I have to admit something. I do care, or some small amount of something is left inside me saying reach out once more and try to find the rest of this horrible puzzle. God only knows what that completed picture will look like, and I mean that literally. I'm not sure I want to see it, but maybe this counseling will be the answer I've been waiting for through the years. I know God, Jesus and the Holy Spirit are real, but I'm just not seeing how *I* could have any value to *them*. That's because of what people did to me, because of what I let people do to me, and because I didn't tell. Three strikes and you're out. The shadows say my chance to tell was then and not now, but my counselor says that is a lie. I guess I am here, at a place where I have no place else to go, so I'll try this. I have nothing to lose and a lot to gain because I do believe in God. I just don't believe in myself. But maybe He still does. So here we go.

My counselor tells me that later, I may need to meet with a friend of hers for some sort of spiritual intervention as the final step in this process, but that getting there will require a lot of preparation. Her friend is an abuse survivor too and lived through a horrific upbringing. In that moment, I asked if I too could go to that fourth dimension world, to that place where her friend can see the shadows and whatever else lives with them. Instantly, I knew that was not a good idea. The angel said to be careful what I wished for, confirming my thoughts. I'm sure she was right, and thinking about that makes me shiver. I fear them.

—

Plato once said *we can easily forgive a child who is afraid of the dark. The real tragedy of life is when men are afraid of the light.* Well, I can be very much afraid of the light because of the shadows. I know that probably doesn't make sense to a lot of people who have not felt that dark presence, so let me try to explain. It's fear again. My thoughts echo with "What is going to happen if I step into the light? What is that light going to show me about myself?" Once again, fear tries to stop me. My counselor says that is how the shadows operate in us, with fear, and it's designed to keep us from God. It's their battle plan. They embody evil of some kind. Years ago, they stole from me the sense of innocent comfort in the world that a child should have. That innocence is the right and sweetness of childhood given to us by God, yet they stole that in my youth and corrupted it. They used me as a lure to corrupt others at the same time and threatened to hurt me if I did not cooperate. Sometimes they hit me afterward anyway just because they could, I guess.

As a result, I have never felt totally safe, either asleep or awake that I can recall. At times, my dreams become nightmares. I suppose they are additional torments to amuse the shadows. The nightmares jar me awake in a cold sweat, and I can still see the images as clearly as if I were still asleep. Thankfully, most of these pictures have faded to someplace where they are no longer visible in my mind. I still worry that new nightmares will come to replace the old ones. How can I make it stop? I can't.

Because of my nights, my days can be exhausting and are sometimes filled with judgments from people who label me as angry and unreachable before even giving me any chance to show them I am a good person inside. Even those I think of as friends do this. They write me off too soon, and the shadows laugh and say things in my mind like, *"Give up, little man; you belong to us, and you will never fit in with them no matter what you do."*

Henry Wadsworth Longfellow described the existence of many abuse survivors perfectly when he said *"Every man has his secret sorrows which the world knows not; and oftentimes we call a man cold when he is only sad."* All too often, I believed the lies the shadows would whisper into my ears, but I am fighting it now, and someday, I will not believe it anymore. Someday.

As to the nightmares, I have clear memories of many of them. Along with images of places where I got hurt in reality, some were bizarre, unreal events. For example, one involved being torn to shreds by a pack of speaking and intelligent dogs. In that dream I was one of them, and they turned on me for sport. To this day, I have no idea what that all really meant, but I can still recall it as clearly as when I dreamed it as a nineteen-year-old kid. It was one of my less graphic dreams too. Did these nightmares come from the shadows?

I suspect they are behind it all. This is the reason I say they are cowards because it's easy enough for them to frighten a little kid or even an adolescent. They have to work harder with adults, and that they do with me on a regular basis. For many of my adult years, I have had dreams of a large white spider in my bed. The thing is huge, probably about six to nine inches across. It had no marks of any kind, just a large white spider. I don't really like spiders, though I respect them in my garden for their role there. Even though my reasoning self knows that the dream spider is not real, I always have to get up, turn on the lights and check to see if the thing is really there. It never is of course.

Regardless, I look and the shadows laugh once more. They succeeded yet again in fooling and tormenting me. It was later that I found out from my first counselor that the image was a reflection of something bad that happened in bed. What that was I don't know, and unfortunately there are too many possibilities.

About a year or so ago, I had another nightmare though I'm not sure that it the right term for it. It got me out of bed and did not come in my sleeping mind like the others had. This thing came in a form that was entirely real and present with me. It appeared as a large dog at the sliding glass door leading from our bedroom to the outside. The animal was beautiful, almost angelic somehow. It looked like a border collie, but its fur was the color of swirled cinnamon and sugar. It had what you may call a "doggie smile" being that contented look dogs present when they are happy. On seeing it at our door, I got out of bed to let it in the house and out of the pouring rain that I was sure it had been desperate to escape. For some reason I was drawn to this animal, thinking it was in trouble and needed to be inside. This woke up my wife, who asked what was going on. I said I was letting this dog in, and she said what dog? When I turned back, it was gone. I thought it had disappeared into the night to find shelter somewhere else. I called it the ginger-dog because of its beautiful fur. Its first appearance is not what frightened me, but that was not the last time I was to see it.

One night shortly thereafter, it returned. The same dog, but this time, it was horrifically different. Its eyes were bright red and turned into flames as it stared at me. The doggy smile was gone. It still wanted me to come to the door and let it in. I would not. I was terrified at the changed image before me. As I stared at it, the spectacle simply vanished. It was as frightening in its second appearance as it was beautiful in the first; everything the same except the doggy smile was gone and it had those flaming eye sockets. I have no idea what it was, but I know it wanted to come into our home. I am grateful something woke my wife the first time to stop me, otherwise, I would have trustingly opened the door the first time to some very bad thing, I'm sure. I'm equally glad for my fear on its second visit. That alone stopped me from inviting evil into our home.

Even with that, evil was to present itself once more. This time, it *would* come inside our home. The last of my nightmare specters happened just recently at this writing. Like the ginger-dog, it was a real form and not something in my dreams. "It" appeared to me as a tall man in the arched doorway that connects our bedroom to the rest of the house.

This time it was not a dream; it was a fully-formed thing in our home that appeared standing upright, in human form as an outline and jet black inside. Its shape was that of a tall man in some sort of old-fashioned cape and wide-brimmed hat. The thing had no face or any other definition inside the form, just solid blackness. A bright light was behind the figure, and it was enveloped in a mist. It was challenging me directly and I have never seen anything like it before.

I guess it knew the white spider trick did not work anymore and the ginger-dog ploy failed as well, so it was upping the ante.

When this shape first appeared, I felt like I was seeing it from the perspective of me at eight or ten years old looking up at him, but that would quickly change. He was a large, imposing, adult male shape. It was, as best I can describe, a fully malevolent thing and clearly not human. It never said a word, but I knew it was there to frighten and challenge me—and it did.

This time, things were different. The shape stirred anger somewhere deep in my soul. I'd had enough and in a flash my anger came to the surface. I was just so tired of these things coming into my life, and I was finally fed up with the images, shadows and nightmares. I challenged it back, and I thank God for giving me the strength to do so. I demanded he identify himself, saying, *"I'm grown up now. You will not hurt me any longer. WHO are you?"*

I don't know if I said that out loud or if I woke my wife, but I could tell the thing heard me clearly. The man, and not the little boy, was challenging it now. By this point, I recall standing defiantly beside our bed. I was finally able to throw the anger inside of me like a spear in the direction of where it rightfully belonged. The thing still never said a word and never showed its face. Coward! I walked toward it, and the shape vanished. It went away and I returned to bed, trembling from the adrenaline mix of anger and fear, but that was done. It has never come back. Coward!

I'm now certain the thing was trying to convince me that it somehow stood between me and the light, which I also now believe was the light of God. I think it wanted to do that because I was working with my first counselor, and it knew I was headed to a place where I would finally be free of it. I'm sure it was trying to trick me again into thinking the light was beyond me, and that I was beyond any hope. So many times before, it had succeeded in convincing me of that. It is a lie I no longer believe, because now I more fully understand that nothing can stand between God and us when we seek His help. My wife, my pastor and my counselors helped me to finally get this.

In fact, when this shape appeared, I had already developed a much stronger understanding of my true relationship with God. My bond with Him was unbreakable, no matter what had worked to frighten me before. This time, I knew the Creator of the Universe was on my side and always had been. God does not care what flaws I have, does not care where I have been or what I have done wrong in the past. He already knows everything, and He only cares where I am going in the future. God has forgiven me. His forgiveness is complete, total, pure and unending.

My guess is that this shadow-figure wanted to reestablish a hold in my mind and heart to destroy the progress I have made. That effort was doomed to failure. Not that I am out of the woods yet, but I am well on my way. Since that time, I've had no more of the nightmares, though I feel the shadows are still there, trying to figure out something new to attempt on me. This all reminded me of Gandalf in *The Lord of the Rings*, when he holds up his staff in the Mines of Morriah and tells the demon *"You shall not pass!"* I am pretty sure a real angel was with me on that summer night in 2010, protecting me and giving me strength to say much the same thing in my own words. It did not pass or find its way into my life again. My hope is these frightening visions, whatever they are, are gone for good. I hope so, and I can only praise God for that. If they return, I know now how to deal with them, and I will.

Chapter FOUR

Hunting is not a sport. In a sport, both sides should know they're in the game.

Paul Rodriguez

MY PATH TO DARKNESS

How did I get here and why did this happen to me? It was several predators who led me into this darkness. I don't know how many times I was taken into dark places, but I remember at least seven of them were involved, maybe more. Predators hunt children; it's that simple. The child does not even know they are in the game or that they are the prey.

Somehow, a predator can spot a child who is hurting, who needs love, and who is not being carefully looked after. Predators exploit that need for love naturally present in all children. They take advantage of a child's innocent nature to corrupt them, and to take what they want when no one is looking. The kid is an object to them, a collection of parts to use as they want and nothing more. Maybe they tell themselves, *"No one protected me so why should I worry about this*

41

kid? He's fair game." Whatever the motivation, they have no problem introducing sadness and evil into a child's life. It's all about them.

For me, the sexual abuse started sometime when I was around five years old. I remember being touched once before that but it was quick, in a swimming pool, and not really traumatic. Whether or not anything else happened before I don't remember. Maybe someday I will.

It was not like we lived in Sodom and Gomorrah. Ours was a small, Midwestern town of around 5,000 residents. It was surrounded by farms, and the city was an hour away by two-lane highway. High school sports were a big deal, and you could count on the noon-whistle going off on-time, every day. I believe the vast majority of the people there were good folks, living decent lives. The ones who got me? Well they operated out of sight and they were probably pretty good at putting on masks of deception in public. My point is, what happened to me does not brand that town with a negative mark in my book. The reality is that this stuff probably happens in every town, regardless of size. It's not just a foreign problem, it's not just an American problem, it's a world-wide problem. It's evil, it's everywhere, and I hate it.

In spite of that presence in my life, I do have happy memories of my childhood there. Many of them. That is, in fact, a big part of the problem I have in trying to write these things down. I feel guilty because in my limited thinking, what happened to me was really nothing when compared to some of the things that I've heard have happened to others. Someone like my counselor's friend had it a lot worse, so what's my problem? That is what I've asked myself many times, and my answer was to just push the hurt away and move on. The thing is, that never worked, because it would always come back with a vengeance. My counselor says that even *one* event of molestation or some other abuse can leave a sad and painful mark that often sets that person on a terrible and often lifelong path. Well it sure did with me. Here I am again, once more without a job, and the enemy is loudly saying;

"Well, you were only ever good for one thing. You're too old for that now, so you might as well just go off and die."

Something in me stubbornly knows that is not an option, and I choose not to go there. Why can't I choose to get rid of the other, stupid, ideas that were planted in my mind as a preteen? The mind of a child is easily manipulated. Once evil finds a way into that child's life, it diminishes the many good things that could have happened to them, even into adulthood. Abuse programmed me early on to follow a destructive path that fed "the great sadness" inside of me, in spite of my best efforts to turn it all around. That is my name for it, and I think it fits. It has been with me as long as I can remember. It also feeds the anger deep inside of me. I have learned to box it up and control that anger most of the time, but it struggles to get free. When it does, I get hurt again.

Long after these things ended in reality for me, my counselor says she can still see the torment they created in my eyes. Sometimes she says I have piercing eyes, and her saying that is so much the opposite of what I am used to hearing from others. I'm used to being told I'm too dense, too slow, not smart enough, lazy, stupid, or things like that. Poets say the eyes are the windows into our soul, and perhaps this angel can see into my soul and look directly at the shadows. I can't imagine what she sees, and I don't want to try.

So it was that through the abuse, evil found a way to attach pain to my spirit. It is like some terrible parasite that is always inside, always gnawing at my conscience. I feel this sadness almost daily on some level, and tormented on a regular basis in my mind at night, even though the physical events ended years ago. I hate what it does to me inside, and maybe that hate just keeps adding fuel to its own fire.

Today, my family and most of the people who know me have no clue that I was molested. I often wonder what they would think of me if they did. Would my family and others finally get why I am sometimes so distant, angry and sad? That would really be nice, but it would be risky too. Would they forgive me? What if they get angry because I didn't speak up sooner? There are so many "what if" questions.

Another confusing part of this puzzle is that I don't know if the people who did things to me had things done to them. For that reason, my counselor says I have to try to forgive them. How is that possible? I don't even know who they were, at least not on any level that I can tap into. Maybe deep down inside somewhere, I do know, but the surface part of my thinking doesn't want to know their identity. Forgive them, me, everything? Why? In order to move on and win this fight? That's what I'm being told has to happen. Well, I had hoped this process would at least be easy with the Spirit as my guide, but it's not. Still, I promised Him I'd try, so I will.

One thing I know about forgiveness is that I need it as well. To be honest, my attempts at this are kind of selfish. How can anyone expect God to forgive them if they are not forgiving? As I understand it, sin is sin. To God there is no difference between molestation, adultery, or simply being mean to another person over some petty issue. In other words, God's perfection is so far from our human imperfection that the differences between the things we do are nothing in comparison to His true nature. My grandmother used to say that only one perfect person has ever walked this earth, being Jesus, of course. I guess that means the best we can do is try to be like Him. Me like

Jesus? How is that even possible after everything that happened and all of the stupid choices I made? This is a puzzle for sure. One thing I learned from my pastor about sin is this. The punishment for it is all the same no matter what the sin, and that punishment is being separated from God, permanently. I don't want that feeling again, so I'll forgive and be forgiven. Well, I'll try.

That is not easy with it all coming to the surface now, and this walk hurts a lot but Jesus is working with my counselor and with me now. My counselor also explained that my feeling any guilt because others suffered something far worse is simply looking at it the wrong way. Abuse is abuse, it is always wrong, and it should never happen. I get that now. It is also clear that the levels of hurt we feel are not a contest to be weighed against what others have had to endure, either. We should not compare something like cancer to abuse, or abuse to blindness. Such experiences are unique to us and painful by any measure.

The damage from being molested, hit and verbally trashed is not something to be ashamed of. I get that too. So the only way is the way forward, as there is still a terrified little boy in my memories who must be set free. We are working on that. My counselor says I have to find the anger imprisoned somewhere inside of me. It feeds off my fear, so I have to face that down somehow. Face it to stomp it, she says.

There is still a terrified little boy in my memories who must be set free. I am an adult now, and it's *my* job to do this. We are working on that, and on finding the pathway to that anger imprisoned somewhere inside of me. The anger feeds off my fear, but at least now I believe that I can find a way to break that chain off of me forever. How that's going to happen is a mystery to me but God knows, and I accept that.

Chapter FIVE

There is no greater sorrow than to recall in misery
the time when we were happy.

Dante

A TARGET IS FORMED

It's not that I really want to quibble with Dante. After all, he wrote *The Inferno* and was a world-renowned thinker, but in this, maybe he had it slightly wrong. He should have said "The time when we were *supposed* to be happy." For a child, home should be a safe and happy place, yet for too many kids that is not the case.

Like so much of the rest of my story, writing about my home life as a kid is not easy because I feel like I am wrongly judging others, and this hurts. The message I get from the Spirit is, *"Keep going son; you need to do this."* OK, I will, but in this moment of writing, I'm angry with you, God, for making me talk about any of this and not just fixing it. My faith is larger than a mustard seed, but I can't move this mountain. Why? You could just make it all go away and heal everything in an instant. So I worry about being angry with God, too. After all, He's God, and He could snuff me out in the blink of an eye and erase any memory of my existence. This ice feels very thin.

My counselor says God's OK with my anger, as I have to figure it out. She tells me that He understands it and won't just wipe me out. It must be true since I'm still here. Writing my story is also tough because now my family relationship is really good, but it sure didn't feel that way to me growing up. Too often, I felt unwanted. When a kid feels that way, it makes it easy for predators to fill the void and provide "love." Kids need to be loved, but for real. It's that simple. That strain on my developing mind of not feeling wanted at home made it easy for predators to get to me, and lie to me to further confuse my thinking.

What they choose to do was in no way my family's fault; none whatsoever. That blame belongs on those men. My counselor has to remind me of that because in some ways, I still blame myself. The rational part of my mind says NO to that idea, but the frightened kid side says YES, it's your fault. It's something we have to sort out. "We" being me, my counselor and the Holy Spirit, and sometimes I just want to stop sorting through a list that seems endless. Ignoring it though, that never got me anything good either, so I have to try.

As for those people, once I was with them, they convinced me they wanted me and would love me. They did want me, of course, but not out of love. Their motive was lust for a child. They were nice enough until they had control over me alone and out of sight. After that, if I didn't cooperate and do what I was told, they got angry. It was very easy for an angry grown-up to control me. If I cooperated, I was told I was "good" and I rarely heard that anywhere else. But good for what?

Every kid gets picked on, and I suspect that every parent has times they were angry and acted inappropriately toward their children.

47

Some people use those things as an excuse to justify bad behavior. More often than not, they'll deny any responsibility for their own choices at the same time, as if it was totally someone else's fault things turned out badly. On the other side, I blamed myself too many years for *everything*, and that's not the right course either. In writing this, it just makes me tear up that I felt unloved, because I know now that was never the case. It was an illusion, another lie, an evil deception that I bought into, and none of it was true. Again, it was the enemy at work with a message of, *"See, little one…they don't love you, but someone else will."* What a total lie!

In my fifth grade school photo, my aunt says I looked like a boy who was mad at the world. I don't see it in the picture, but she does and so do others. She also says, *"We all thought it was so funny how you would storm around and have fits over little things."*

I don't believe that comment was intentionally mean at all. It was just not well thought out. Why was it that no one asked what makes an eleven-year-old so angry at the world, since that's what they saw in me? That frustrates me a lot to this day, that no adult in my life apparently ever put those pieces together. Maybe they did and I don't know, but somewhere deep inside of me, there is still a cry waiting and wanting to be heard:

"Where were you grown-ups? You were supposed to protect me! I don't want to inflict guilt on you now, I just want to know why no one figured out that a ticked off little kid has something more going on inside than just growing pains."

It's just not natural that children are frustrated and angry for years at a time. When a child is that way, along with being sad and distant, there is a reason for it. Some responsible adult should not be afraid to ask…why?

– Scrambled Signals –

I cannot go into details of the events, those times and places of sexual abuse that led me to feeling unlovable growing up. I won't do it, put my own words to images I do not want to see anymore. Besides, I don't know how many times I was "gotten" or how many people were really involved. I know it was mostly men, and there are fragments of memories lost to me. Spaces of time that don't exist in my mind. The only thing that does is the beginning and end of specific events, and of course the images that visit my dreams at night. The middle, those details of specific and graphic things—I don't see most of them, and I don't want to. What I can see is more than enough.

Other things are less difficult to talk about, like misunderstanding things at home or school, but even that is not easy really, either. At least not until I can sort this all out, because this counseling has shown me that I have it wrong anyway. I blame myself. Sometimes I blame others, but ultimately it comes back to me. The enemy says GUILTY, and I buy into it. He used things to distort my view of the world as a kid, because it is very easy to fool a child. That's how the enemy operates. He took things and made them something totally different from truth in my child's mind. Perhaps if I talk about some of these things in general, then maybe I can show how the Spirit is helping me rebuild that puzzle into a true picture.

So to do that, I can talk more about some of my relationships with family growing up. I still really do not understand my relationships with my grandparents. Just like with the rest of my family, I have many good memories of them. In their own ways, they all loved me, but what happened when I was a preteen made it impossible for me to know that at the time.

Of all my grandparents, my dad's dad was the only one who never got angry with me, not even once. I can't picture him getting angry about anything or with anyone. Anger was just not a part of who he was. My paternal grandfather was a farmer of gentle and good humor. While not highly educated, as formal learning goes, he was clearly a scholar of the land and equally of the Bible's teachings about the golden rule. I'll always be able to hear his quiet voice in the calm places of my mind where even the shadows can't go. I can still hear him telling me stories of the chicken hawk that would circle and circle as his hand moved above me, and then—gotcha! That story always made me laugh no matter how many times I heard it. I never knew when the hawk would get me as his hand constantly circled above my head while he told stories of the sneaky birds who stole his chickens away. The suspense was a thrill ride in itself. With him, I felt safe even from that scary chicken hawk. I got scared but in a good way. In those moments, I knew and felt true love.

It adds another sad and twisted element to my story to note that later, I learned that the term "chicken hawk" refers to men who seduce and hurt young boys for their own enjoyment. I heard that… you're my little "chicken" kid. Regardless, that use of the term does not take away what my paternal grandfather gave me. His words and the love in them are still more powerful than anything imprinted on me by the predators. I can still see his gentle smile in my mind, where I have it locked in a safe place in my heart along with other kind thoughts such as his wonderful stories. They are a lifeline for me, especially now, going through counseling. As I write and recall these long neglected memories, they provide a gentle counterpoint to everything else I've had to write so far. They remind me that at least one more person did love me completely and without conditions applied to it.

My dad's mother, on the other hand, seemed grumpy much of the time and more easily annoyed by me. Yet even in her grumpiness, I still remember she made the best homemade bread and I loved our meals at her table. In her later years, I had a great relationship with her, and we shared many good, loving conversations. I guess she forgave me for the annoyances I caused her as a little kid, and I equally forgave her for the grumpy thing. Before she passed, I was happy to find genuine love and approval in her eyes. She left this life with each of us knowing that we loved each other. How stupid it was of me not to understand how much they both really loved me sooner than I did. These memories are anchors for me now. I did not even realize I had them until the Spirit showed me the love there. I have to hold tight to those while I try to unscramble the rest of this story.

My mom's parents were not really all that different. They, too, came from farming families. My maternal grandmother, however, came from a home where her parents expected all of their children to get a college education. She did so, in teaching of course, as that was what most women studied in those days. My maternal grandfather had a much harsher upbringing. His father wandered away from the family much of the time, and eventually he stayed away too long. My great-grandfather died alone, miles away from their farm, off in another state. I have no idea what shadows haunted him either, but I am sure he had to deal with them too.

In spite of that, my grandfather managed to get his formal education in teaching as well. He and my grandmother went on to become prominent citizens of the town, the kind of people others would greet first with polite deference if they were not good friends of the family. They were often generous with their money to the town, contributing respectable sums to local charities. As the town elite, they had standards and respectability.

For me, somehow, it almost always felt like I did not fit into that ideal picture. (Guess where I got that idea?) Into their world, my birth was an unplanned event. It was a difficult pregnancy for my mom. My grandmother frequently reminded me over the years that my mother almost died when I was born, saying, *"You almost killed your mother."*

God knows I hated hearing that, and I heard it too many times. It was not said with anger or even with malice, just sort of matter-of-fact, but still without any regard for how such words made me feel. It should not have ever been said to me at all. What kid needs to know that or have that kind of label put on them?

By the time I was born, my mom's parents had already come to dislike my father, and they did so for the rest of their lives. It felt like their feelings toward him sometimes transferred onto me. After all, I was born after they came to see him as bad so I must be "bad" too. My birth was not planned, and I was a living reminder of my father's sins. While I was never directly called a mistake, sometimes unsaid words can be spoken just by a look of disapproval. I got the message. Often the word "accident" *was* used about me when people didn't know that I could hear them, and hearing it directly or indirectly is the same thing. I came to believe that I was a "mistake" that should not have come into this world, but my counselor taught me that God doesn't make mistakes. He created me and planned for me to be in this world, just like He planned for me to be set free and placed on this new path.

– The Good Old Days –

From the time I was eight or so, we would spend the summers at my maternal grandparents' home. During those times, I have happy memories as my grandmother did try hard to entertain us. She would set up "tents" with bed sheets in the backyard and make creative lunches. When I think on these memories and on the less pleasant ones, it shows me now what I got were different signals that as a kid I had no way to intellectually sort out.

I grew into the artistic type kid, much more so than my athletic brother. My art was something I could do alone, so that appealed to me and I enjoyed it. I didn't have to worry about making anyone else unhappy by failing, by drawing a stupid picture or writing a poem that stunk. I could just do it for me. In my artistic world I was also mostly out of the line of fire, or so I believed.

One time, I walked to a store downtown and bought this toy that had stickers of people and objects you could paste or re-paste into little magnetic scenes that also came in the box. I was thrilled when I found it. It had so many possibilities and worlds my imagination could explore for hours without bothering anyone, getting under foot, and making people annoyed just because I knew I would be out of the way. I could not wait to get it home and play in those imaginary worlds.

When I brought it into the house, I was so excited that I had to tell about it. That was a big mistake as all hell broke loose with my announcement. In a flash, all of the adults were ticked off at me again. In the same instant my joy turned into fear once more, and my excitement into sadness.

"You're too old for that!" were the searing words yelled at me by someone in the room. I don't remember who it was, but it doesn't matter, because the rest of the adults seemed to be in total agreement with that opinion judging by their looks and mumbled comments. This toy that just a few minutes before had brought me joy and excitement now turned into a weight in my hands, as all eyes targeted me with more disappointment. What did I do wrong now? I remember the moment clearly, feeling absolutely confused, and for what? Buying a toy with money that I had earned myself.

Honestly, you would have thought I brought home a porn magazine. And what was the problem anyway? I was going to have fun with it and not cause problems for anyone, so really what was the problem? I don't get why a toy mattered enough to generate such angry disapproval. So what if the box said it was meant for a four-to six-year-old and I was maybe eight. Big deal, my imagination could put it to good use. That displeasure made me cower and want to go away again, which is what I did often. This time, it made me angry, too. I hated them for treating me that way, all of them. I didn't do anything wrong but felt bad again just for being there. I see now it was the enemy at work again.

I just walked silently to the back bedroom that served as my place to be alone. I don't know how long it took me to open the toy and play with it but eventually I did, and I had fun with it too. I didn't care if they disapproved of it or of me. That toy became a friend, and *it* didn't judge me. Of course, it didn't because it was really just cardboard, rubber and plastic. In my imagination, however, it was a friend that sparked good thoughts in me and provided an escape.

No one ever mentioned the toy again, but what was said, was said, and I never forgot it. Besides, no one except my grandmother noticed the drawing tablet and colored pencils that I also bought that day. I guess the others were too focused on the stickers toy. Later, I used the tablet and colored pencils to draw very lifelike animals or people from magazine pictures. In those days, I didn't know who Bob Hope was, but I drew his caricature from a picture I saw in an old magazine. I also looked at pictures of animals and once drew a pretty lifelike face of a tiger. How many eight- or nine-year-olds can do that? Draw a lifelike face of a tiger from just looking at a photograph?

My grandmother was genuinely delighted and recognized them right away, with great praise as well. That, for me, is another good memory of her for which I am thankful. At the same time, no one else noticed the drawings or said anything if they did. So once again, I got mixed signals and the enemy was more than happy to use that to his advantage. I stopped drawing not long after that summer and have not picked up a paintbrush or colored pencils in the years since except when I had to in school. Even so, I want to draw and paint again. One day, I will pick up where the eight-year-old me left off, when I am done with this, and I will be good at it again too.

– Little Wimp –

It was my artistic side that probably incurred my maternal grandfather's greatest level of displeasure in me. That artsy stuff was simply not a "boy thing" to him. It was yet another dimension of my personality that he didn't understand and didn't care for.

It is hard to describe my relationship with my mom's father, and I am trying hard not to make him sound like a bad person. He wasn't some monster, and he was not at all like the predators. To them, I was just an object. I would describe my grandfather as a somewhat quiet man. He also seemed strict, maybe because of the abuse out-side of our home had created an unnatural fear in me, as others in my family do not remember him that way. I would like to think that early on, he tried to teach me more of what he thought boys should really know, but I have no memory of anything like that at all. None. I remember more often than not just being afraid of him. I was fearful of the consequences that, right or wrong, I was sure were to follow if I didn't get everything perfect *and* get it right the first time. I had learned that criticism and labels are what followed failure.

"Stupid, lazy little bastard."

My grandfather didn't say that as far as I can recall, but I heard and learned those words somewhere. They became a label that I wore inside. I was not stupid or lazy, and certainly not the last word either, but that phrase is what the shadows would whisper in my mind at night. It was part of their well-crafted evil routine for my world on days when I didn't get something right.

I remember once my grandfather had sought out where my brother and I were playing. He said something to my brother like "Come on, let's go practice fishing," using my brother's name — and only his name. It could have been golf or catch or anything else. The point is I was sitting right there and was clearly not to be included. I knew it, and I didn't really want to be anyway. It hurt nonetheless hearing that.

At other times I did go with them, but fear stopped me from trying, and I guess my grandfather just stopped trying as well. I don't really blame him for it, and I was happy to be free of that expectation. He had grown up way too early on that farm, but used his survival skills to become a talented businessman. Seeing that a child was hurting and fearful was just not something he could do, for whatever reason. I was learning survival skills too, and things had already set me up to accept kindness and love elsewhere by the time that summer came along. Evil had taken advantage of both our lives.

Later on, he and I would come to a sort of mutual respect for each other, even love. He didn't leave this world thinking I hated him as I didn't, nor did he hate me in his last years either. I wish things would have been different much sooner, but we were to part lives in a good place. It could be God was teaching us both something about forgiveness. Before that, however, things between my maternal grandfather and I would get much worse, as the next section illustrates.

– Fishing Trips –

For years, my mom's father had a fishing cabin in the Canadian backwoods. He owned it jointly with his buddies. My uncle got to go with him and take my cousins along too, but my grandfather's "rule" was that grandsons were only welcome if their father brought them, and my father was obviously not going to be welcome at the cabin ever. Funny how that rule worked. It was custom-made to rule out my brother and I, or at least me is what I think now. I'm sure if I had not been around, that rule would not have even been made.

So it was during the summer when I was ten or eleven, maybe, my mom (and maybe my aunts and grandmother) somehow talked my grandfather into taking my brother and I along to the cabin. Before going, I got to learn how to cast for fish by practicing in my grandparents' backyard. It didn't help, as there is a lot more to fishing then just casting, but no one showed me the rest.

As for the cabin, now that was a really cool place. Located deep in the Canadian woods and surrounded by huge lakes, it had been a general store built from logs in the 1800s. I loved the woods, but I hated sitting in that boat all day. I hated more that every single lunch and every single dinner were, you guessed it, fish…always fish. I hated fish then and I still do. Breakfast, on the other hand, consisted of lots of wonderful pancakes my uncle or grandfather made. At least I could eat my fill of those without anyone's scorn, and they were really delicious too.

I mention the scorn about eating because shortly after the drive up started, the first troubles did too. My grandfather had yanked a box of cookies out of my hand. I was grazing like any little kid would do when left unchecked, and he ripped it out of my hands. No correcting words, like that is enough. Instead, he just snatched it from my hands, called me some name under his breath and turned back around to the front. It was dead quiet in the car for several miles. From the start, that clearly set the tone for rest of the trip. I'd done it again, whatever "it" was, and this was just the beginning. The rest of the drive up and overnight stay in International Falls was uneventful, thankfully.

We got to the cabin the next day, and I loved the whole rustic look and smell of the woods. Once we made it out onto the lake the next morning for a day of fun, if you want to call it that, I could never catch anything while it seemed like everyone else around me kept reeling them in. No one tried to teach me to do things differently to catch fish when we were in the boat, but I was probably not receptive anyway. I did not want to be there.

One evening after our return for the day, I asked my grandfather if I could paddle the canoe around in the little cove by the cabin. It was only around three in the afternoon, and the sun would not go down for hours. He was clearly not pleased with that request, but he let me go anyway, with the warning that I was only going to get in trouble because the water and winds were too rough.

Really? THEN DON'T LET THE KID GO IF YOU CARE ABOUT HIM! To this day, I want to shout those words at that image and his reply to my request. Honestly, I don't think he did care in that moment anyway.

As my usual luck would have it, my canoe did get blown over to a small island where I became stranded, not being strong enough to paddle even the short distance back to the cabin. I waved the paddle at those on shore and called as loudly as I could to signal I needed help. As was often the case, no one seemed to notice. My grandfather and someone else then got into one of the motorboats and headed out to do a little more fishing. They just cruised right past me, probably no more than fifty feet from where I was stuck on my little island calling to them for help. I know they saw me, too, but they did not acknowledge me in any way, they just kept going. It felt like a giant middle finger sailing past. Maybe an hour later, they came back and stopped to tow me to shore, with some annoyance expressed from my grandfather in his eyes, words, and tone once more. I'd screwed up again, and I could clearly tell that he was angry again at me for it. I got another look that said, *"I didn't want you here in the first place."*

Well, so what? I didn't want to be there either, and that was not my fault! YOU were the responsible adult and I was a kid. Whether you wanted me there or not, we were stuck with each other. Inside, I was just as angry with him as he seemed to be at me. I was tired of trying and failing, and tired of knowing he didn't want me there. It wasn't my idea, but I was held accountable simply by just existing on that trip. I was also tired of being kicked around with no one saying anything about it. It was not my fault I was born or that you hate my dad. Why was I expected to act like a grown-up when the grown-ups weren't doing so? Those are the thoughts that go through my mind now, as I have to talk about this.

There was to come a single moment where I thought I'd finally found something that would redeem me in my grandfather's eyes, since I could not catch fish or do anything else right. Someone had dumped garbage on the lot where the cabin stood. That pile of trash rightfully ticked him off when we pulled up, as we would have to get rid of it. Being a curious kid, I poked through it and found an envelope with a name and address of what could be the owner of the trash. My grandfather's friend told me that was pretty smart thinking for a boy. My grandfather was unimpressed and didn't say a word. Couldn't they use this to track down the people who dumped the stuff there, I asked. Not one word, he just turned around and walked away.

It was just more mixed signals, and my brief hope of redemption was totally trashed. Well, at least I was by the trash heap that time. The trip lasted a week. My brother and I were never invited back. My brother would have been welcomed because he loved the whole thing. I'd never go back there unless someone made me do it. Thankfully, no one did. The adults must have talked about it all after our return and realized it was a disaster too.

A year later, my father took my brother and I up to the same area. Just down the road from my grandfather's cabin was a small rustic resort where we stayed. Honestly, that trip was a lot more fun. We had an Indian guide named Alfred who was the nicest man, gentle in his nature, and the kind of person who always wore a smile. I did catch fish that time too. Alfred showed me how to do it. For some reason, there was one fish in particular I felt we had to put back. I don't know why, but we just had to. I told Alfred and he smiled at me kindly. He told me if I felt that way, it was for a reason and that we should let the fish go. He didn't think it was stupid at all, or make any hurtful comments. Alfred and I took it to the lake, and with a gentle shake from Alfred, the fish revived once back in the water and swam off happily, I'm sure.

It was in Alfred's boat that I felt my first real physical touch from an angel. I was at the front of the boat enjoying the day this time and happily describing a fish. Like most people, I had my hands up showing how long it was while my fishing rod lay across my knees. At that moment, I got a bite and the rod quickly pulled off my lap, going into the water before I could stop it. I stretched out trying to retrieve it, but a firm hand grabbed my shoulder and pulled me back to my seat. Darn, I almost had it…that was close! Well, maybe not, but I wanted to know who had pulled me in.

At that point, I realized no one was close enough to do so. I still protested that I felt the hand. Alfred just smiled a big grin. He must have known it was an angel, and later, I'd figure that out too. With the loss of my fishing pole, I still did not get into trouble and no one was angry with me or yelled at me or called me names. Well, that was different, and it felt great.

I didn't even get into trouble later when I had wandered off into the woods that I loved. The Mounties, my father, and brother along with Alfred, had come looking for me. They found me, and again, while I did not get yelled at, I did get a good talking to in a way a kid should get one. That trip was truly one of those times where I could see my father was genuinely worried about me and that he loved me.

As for Alfred, I'm sure he must be gone to live with Jesus by now. I can't wait for the day till I get to meet him again. I wonder if Alfred was really an angel put there just for me, and was the one who pulled me back into the boat. I guess I'll find out when I get to heaven because I know he's there. I love you, Alfred, for all of that, and I can't wait to see you again. It was a good trip with my father and brother, too. While my relationship with my dad was often strained, it wasn't on that trip, and it was a true blessing in my young life.

My father and I would have more difficult times ahead throughout my teenage years and into my college days. At one point, I stopped talking to him for a period of close to two years. That stubbornness ended in me later on in graduate school when I had another serious bout with thoughts of suicide. I had decided not to take that step, and I also decided it was time to try to set things right again. Today, my relationship with my dad is on solid ground and I would not trade it for anything. We love each other and that's real, as God intended it to be all along.

It all illustrates very well why my stepfather had been so important in my life as I went from being a preteen into adolescence. Unlike my natural father, at the time, he acted like a dad and loved me for who I was until the day he died. It's like he could see what God sees in me, the person I did not see at the time. I'm certain now that my stepfather would have helped me turn all of this around had he known what had happened and been aware of the traps and programming snares that had strongholds on my thinking in those days. I was not even aware of them, anyway, and didn't know what it was I needed to explain. I just knew that inside, something about being alive simply hurt. My experiences had me confused, but I really did not think there was anything wrong with the sexual stuff. It didn't make sense to me, but it seemed that everyone acted like sex was just a game anyway. Because my future stepfather was strong, honest and loving, I was afraid to tell him about my confusion even if I could have found the words. The seeds of fear and mistrust had been firmly rooted in me. Many "what ifs" came into my mind when I considered the idea of telling him. What if he saw me as bad? What if he got angry with me? Those thoughts led me to believe that rejection would quickly follow if I spoke up, and I did not want to risk losing our connection, as it was one of the few good ones with an adult in my life. There you go, yet another lie of the enemy, and I had accepted it.

That fear kept me silent and evil had won again. The good news is that I did reconcile with my natural father. I have come to believe he has changed for real. I now know that he loves me too. I love him as well, and our relationship is better than it ever was. Somehow, God had reminded a very stubborn me that forgiveness is something we do for ourselves as much as we do it for others, but we need to do it to be really free. I am so glad that with my dad, I was able to forgive and move on to being close to him as a son.

I'm learning that we have to forgive others who mend their ways, as that's what God does for us. However, repentance is confusing to me. Do we forgive people who have not repented? I don't know if the predators have done that. My memories of them tell me it's doubtful they ever have or will repent of that sin. Yet I think the answer is yes, because on the cross, Jesus forgave those around Him who had no intention of repenting. For that reason, we forgive them and turn it over to God. He certainly knows as well as I do that there is a lot for which I need forgiveness. So I still swim in this murky confusion while that lifeline hangs above my head, within my grasp. I have not taken hold of it yet, and haven't yet forgiven the people who started all of this in me, or forgiven myself either for letting them do it and not saying anything. The angel, my awesome counselor, says I'll get there. We have to work on that, but at least I am trying to believe it now, and am very happy with the relationship I have today with my father. He is my dad now. I am happy to be with him and look forward to seeing him. I don't care what his faults are, and I would not break our new bond for anything. I think this is the start of something big for me, thanks to my new relationship with my Father in Heaven too.

Just as I now have with my dad, I also now have a great relationship with the other members of my family. I love them dearly, and I have lots of good memories of them in my mind to dwell on, if I need to dwell on something. Of course they still tease me, and I still get annoyed, but their teasing is not done with the malice that I believe was once there. With so much other stuff happening in my little world during my growing up years, I could have easily storyboarded some of the teasing episodes into something bigger than they ever were. Storyboarding is taking something small and turning it into a major motion picture in our mind. How many times do we do that with things that just don't matter? I've done it many times.

Regardless, it does not matter now. My siblings and I have a great relationship and I love them. Nothing from the past is going to change that. I will not let it. The shadows are no longer in control and they shall not destroy that relationship I have with my brother and sisters today. Realizing this, I think, is part of the healing, and it's truly a blessing. My counselor says that when I'm done with all of this, my "great sadness" will go away forever too, just like in the book called *The Shack*. As with everything else she's told me, I believe it's true. I am so looking forward to that, to the day when I will finally be free of this sadness and the deep hold it has on my life. Probably the toughest thing for me to think on is that my siblings, like my parents and the rest of my family, have no idea about the cumulative events in my story that brought me here. They do not know about the events outside of our home that sent me so many mixed messages and pulled me in too many directions, things that I could not fight or understand at the time.

Right now, I plan to keep it that way simply because I see no point in inflicting that hurt on their lives at this time. My rational side tells me it serves no good purpose, that too many years have passed. Nothing they do or say could change anything. It would only hurt them and make them sad for something that was not their fault or mine. I can see no benefit in that, none whatsoever. That being the case, there is no point in letting my family in on a secret that will only hurt them. They might even argue that I should not make that choice for them, but all this happened to me, so it is my choice.

Yet another part of me speaks in a voice that is loud and clear. It says I need to tell them. It says I have to show them what I've written here. To tell or not to tell is yet another choice I hate to think about, and I suppose it's another thing I have to ask the angel about. I am sorry, I am so sorry, and I have to stop again. The tears are back.

—

In writing for the next session, my thoughts are that evil is really good at twisting our lives when it has a stronghold. I look at all of the things I wrote above and still don't understand it and wonder if I am even seeing anything clearly.

Evil is still trying to do the same thing now as I try to tell my story, trying to twist my thoughts. I have to fight to keep myself from hating people all over again, those whom I've tried to forgive. To do that, I have people in my life now who know about this stuff and support me. I also have my counselor and God to help me fight. So to evil and the shadows, I say this: I love my family. Nothing you pull up from the past will hit me now like it used to, and nothing you say to me will diminish that love. So what if they made mistakes? I did too. I fell for all of your garbage before, but only because I was a little kid and easily manipulated. I'm not playing anymore, got that?! My counselor says we'll find all of your hiding places and shine a light in there to erase you. You will disappear as quickly as a flash, and you can go back to the darkness from which you came.

There is more I have to write, but I just can't do it now. God is again telling me to give it a rest, and I'm happy to obey. My mind is tired and I ache inside. I'm sure in the end, I'll say it's a good ache, but in this moment, it hurts telling about all of this. I hope it ends soon; please God.

Author's Note

The next chapter covers a pivotal moment in my journey. After decades of being afraid to speak, I would be silent no more. In our next session, I would tell my counselor the details of what happened. It would be the first time that I ever actually spoke out loud about it to anyone. *On that day, God gave me back my voice.* As for the details, they are not here, as I don't need to see them in print anymore. The important thing is what God did in me on that day and not what the predators did to me years before. My life was about to change forever.

The journal continues.

Chapter SIX

Evil endures a moment's flush and then leaves
but a burnt up shell.

Elise Cabot

INVISIBLE BOY, VOICE RESTORED

I am about to enter into what I expect will be the worst phase of counseling. I have to tell my counselor what I remember. This means no more hiding my eyes from her, but finding and actually *saying* the words to describe what happened. It will be the most difficult conversation I'll ever have.

Of course, I have to write first because that is what I do, but this time, it'll lead to more than just reading my words. It means expanding on them too and that scares me. Some of this I've never even said aloud to myself, but here's the deal: everything else I've experienced so far, including the anger, the shadows, the difficulties in relationships and the problems I had with my people—they are all the result of these "events." So today, we have to go back to those people and places and try to let it out somehow.

Write it down! Those words ring in my mind as I sit here, still feeling like the leftover shell of some kid used up long ago and nothing more, trying to get ready to speak with my counselor. That thinking is just my worry coming out as I approach this counseling session. It is worry that is trying to stop me from going. Well I *am* going. How will this change my fear to freedom? I don't know, but my promise to the Spirit was that I'd cooperate. A promise is a promise, and I promised my obedience to Him.

Talking out loud is a necessary step, my counselor says. It's something I must do, so here goes. The sexual abuse started when I was around five years old, and by the time I turned nine, others would find their way into my life. How many people were really involved is a mystery to me, and it's not an answer I want to find. As I entered the fourth grade, I knew well how to do things no kid that age should have any idea about. I had also become a friend to anger and fear, and in that, my innocence had been burned up by evil and consumed. Because of it, I can't remember a time when I was not afraid of anger coming at me from one source or another if I didn't cooperate. In that time, my hands began to tremble, and if fear was very intense, the shaking got significantly worse. As I grew up, people assumed it was drugs or too much caffeine or just plain cowardice in me. They had a clue what the real source was. The shakes just became part of my daily life, along with the labels attached to me by others and myself.

I refer to those times that I was taken (or tricked) away from public view as events. I call them that because I don't like to say other words that are more accurate like rape or molestation. There are gaps in my memories too, with only a few deposits of fleeting images as reference points. They are snapshots of single moments in time, or short movies that play in my thoughts. Places, events, and people whose faces I cannot see even though the rest of their physical presence is clear enough, along with what they did. These things seem complete and yet incomplete at the same time, validations of something but not the whole thing. Along with the people and events, I remember a shed, several houses, a car, and a place out in the country by the river. That's all, but it's more than enough.

Those pictures anchor sadness inside of me. The sadness is part of my existence, and it always has been in one form or another as far back as I can remember. It was there when I was little, it was there when I was a teenager, and it has stayed chained to me as an adult. It is even with me as I am writing this. There are days or maybe a couple of weeks when the shadows do not come into my dreams at night. It's a kind of break from the sadness, but inside, I know they will always return. They always do. They are never far away. That is still true for me even today. For years, they had me convinced I was somehow made for "that" or worse, and that I somehow *deserved* it. Through the help I'm getting now, my understanding gets sharpened that these thoughts are just lies I was taught. I have not shed them completely from my belief system yet, but I am getting a whole lot closer to doing that. It is a kind of hope for me. Hope for an escape from this is something I've never had before, and I'll take it. It is my lifeline. I remember reading once in school a saying that went like this: *"Never deny someone hope; it may be all they have left."* Hope has found a home in me now.

During the day, the battle in my mind continues because even then, the shadows use ordinary things as a chance to whisper reminders in my ear. Something as mundane as walking past a house that looks like the one in my old neighborhood where some of the abuse happened provides an opening in my thoughts when the shadows will say:

"Remember the shed behind that one house...and what you did there? What you let them do there? Remember??"

Yeah, I remember parts well enough, memories of something. The shadows show me just enough so that I don't forget that something happened. I want to know the rest, but at the same time, I don't want to see any of it. My counselor says the memory gaps are my mind's way of protecting me from things I'm not ready to see yet and could not handle right now. I don't get how that is protecting me at all. One of the shadow tricks happens when I see parents playing with and loving their children, as good parents should do. My thoughts say *"You were bad, so you missed out on good times like that,"* which is another lie because I had good times like that as a kid. I really did. Some of those times were messed up by one adult or another being angry, but not all of them. The shadows want me to believe a lie that none of it was good, and to believe that I was never really good either. Lies. It is one of the many terrible side effects of abuse. It's what happens when we learn to accept ungodly beliefs about ourselves. Such things have a way of punching holes in what should be good memories, like letting the air out of a balloon. I still have the balloon in my hand but it's not quite the same. It's an empty shell.

That's what the shadows do to me and to others like me, I'm sure. They are very good at it. As a consequence of their games and the events themselves, I grew into a confused and difficult adulthood. I became angry or judgmental about unimportant things, and people too often found me hard to understand or accept but easy to reject. I came to accept that rejection was normal, at least for me.

Now I'm told I must try to put the pieces together into a timeline, more or less. As a starting point, she wants me to deal with the memories that I can see clearly. Through talking about them, we will be

71

able to get to the images that hide behind a dark fog. If it were not for the clear memories, I'd have concluded long ago that I was just a mental case and nothing more. Oddly enough, I remember that in the seventh grade, my health teacher told us, "*Seven percent of you kids will grow up with mental illness.*"

That was a stupid thing for a teacher to say, and I sat there in junior high thinking she already knew I'd be one of them. As for memories hidden in that fog, I don't want to see them clearly, but again I know that is part of the process. My counselor says we have to do it, and I trust her. Besides, I get the feeling God will be lovingly annoyed with me if I don't do this. I am very sure there is going to be a lot of unpleasantness down this road, and I fear going there.

Sometime in my early life, I learned how to disassociate. My understanding is that it is a coping mechanism children learn in order to deal with painful events that are beyond their comprehension. I somehow figured out how to do it, to separate my mind from my physical self and go to a safe place. For me, that safe place was a world run by very smart and kind house cats. I love cats, and in this world I was the cat leader. It was very futuristic, like some *Star Wars* planet. In that place others would come to me for advice or justice. I was always fair. More importantly, I was loved there without conditions. In my real world, love often had other requirements attached to it.

If someone asked me now to explain when or how the dissociation came about, I'd have to say I really do not understand how people learn to do that. I didn't even know it had a name until my counselor asked me if I ever went to a "safe place" as a little kid and she explained dissociation to me. I was well practiced at it by the time I was in college.

While I have not been to the cat world in years, I can still drift totally away in my thoughts today and think about things I love, such as gardens. Unfortunately, there are times when my mind used to drift to bad things to play over and over again in my head, like a YouTube clip where someone keeps hitting the restart button. But in this area, too, counseling has really helped me. I've discovered how to hit the stop button and cast those things away. Learning about this dissociation thing was another real turning point. I had known for years there was that safe place in my mind, but never knew or even suspected that the practice had a name or that others did the same thing. Knowing this makes it feel less abnormal.

It was during a recent *Oprah* program, of all things, that I realized how much my own experience mirrors that of so many other guys. Having missed the first showing, I got up at 1:30 a.m. to watch the rebroadcast. From that television program, I learned that many boys are abused, perhaps as many as one in five or six, and that I have shared a collection of mixed feelings with thousands of them. All my life, I have heard some people say it's not that big of a deal when it comes to boys and sexual abuse. Some people would say utterly stupid things like, *"So what? Boys like sex anyway, so it's different for them than it is with girls."* I will never understand that thinking. It is a big deal for thousands of men and boys today, and it hurts for a long time after the abuse stops.

– Finding Invisible Chains –

I will not identify the town where it all happened, as that serves no purpose. It's sufficient to say that it was just one of those small towns where most of the people probably figured it was a safe place to live, work, and raise your kids.

We lived in the middle of town. Even at a very young age, I wandered around freely with my best friend. As little kids, he and I would sometimes go downtown. It was a short walk of maybe five or six blocks, or we would ride our bikes around the neighborhood and go play up by the water tower or in a little park nearby. I can't imagine anyone letting a five-year-old just wander like that today, but that was our world. Nothing that I recall ever happened to me in the places where we played, but I wonder if someone first noticed me there. I also wonder how they even picked me out to begin with? As a side note, I am trying desperately to assemble all of this, but I know God is here and I have real help now to put it all together somehow.

During one time, I vividly remember finding a condom in a shed behind someone's house. With equal clarity, I remember already knowing what it was and how it was used. During the session, my counselor asked me, *"What five-or six-year-old knows what a condom is unless someone showed him?"*

I had never put that together before; it simply never clicked in my mind until she said that. She's right; little kids don't automatically know what condoms are, yet I did when I found one in that shed. That I remember as clearly as a bell's ring. I had been there before and for some reason, I was in that shed again. This time I was not alone. From the spot by the window, he pulled me into a dark corner. He did what he wanted to do and got what he wanted from me, threatening me if I didn't cooperate. He then threatened once more when he was finished. After that, I'm left alone. Somewhere behind him during all of this, I bet the shadows were laughing. Right now, as I'm writing this to read for my counselor, I clearly hear another voice hissing in my ear, saying:

"Useless little _____; this was all you were good for."

I won't repeat all the words, but it's like the shadows are still telling me now what they must have said back then. They want to make writing this difficult for me, and it is. That's all I see now and the image slams shut to darkness again. I'm glad for that. I so much *do not* want to see any more of that day or that shed and him.

Another thing is happening as I am writing this. My rational, grown-up self is sitting here saying this can't be real, none of it. Who would do that to a five-year-old? Yet my memories are there. Where did they come from and what little kid knows what a condom is? I suppose my counselor and I are going to have to sort this out. There were more experiences from my preteen years in different places, and at least three that I can think of. There is no need for me to describe them or what happened there now, as I will talk to her about it. Right now, I don't want to think about that shed or any of those places anyway.

When I told my counselor this, I stubbornly said that I didn't want to turn the pages back any further to see what else is there. I'm starting to do that with her now, and I recall more details, more getting tricked, getting used and hit to ensure my silence. God knows I hate doing this, but I have to. I'm pretty certain all of the events are connected because there is a common figure in most of them. I won't identify him because this man is dead and God will deal with him. I will never say who he was now, except to say he was *not a member of our family*. It saddens me that others have to live with the layer of incest added onto their abuse, too. It's all just wrong, no matter what the source.

– Never Tell –

There are chains that bind victims of abuse. One of them is manip-ulation. Before any victim of abuse can ever start talking, they have to get past one key idea planted in them by the abusers. "Don't tell!" Those words were said to me as angry commands to reinforce their control. It's weird how I can remember the anger in their eyes and not the rest of their faces. Their eyes and words had control. One thing I've learned about myself is that I was the kind of kid who needed affection, and most of all, one who craved approval. Yet isn't that what every kid naturally wants and needs? My counselor told me that my personality test showed those two traits as being the strongest in me, but isn't that normal for a kid? Again, it's like evil somehow took something that is normal and used it against me. When abusers told me I was good, those words filled a need that today I cannot under-stand. It makes me feel shame again, and guilt for being so stupid because I fell for that lie.

There was a third facet to how they controlled me, and that was with fear. If I didn't cooperate, I got hit. Their phony words had filled a desperate need in me yet if I hesitated, then that weapon would come out. Through it all, I am sure the shadows laughed. They had gotten deep into my soul and I was further corrupted with every new episode. In one way, I am lucky, far luckier than many others. For me, these events did not happen daily or weekly. It was off and on for some four years. It doesn't matter how many times it happened. As my counselor says, one event or one hundred, it's all bad and can scar a kid deeply. That part I understand well. One thing I know for sure; as I approached my eighteenth birthday, thoughts of suicide came to my mind. Once I was an adult, what would I be good for?

It would not be the last time I had those thoughts, but I thank God that He had different ideas and somehow kept me from going there.

Early on in counseling, I had to ask the question of why me. Why? And how could I fall for such lies? My counselor told me the shadows couldn't care less about me, they wanted to hurt God. She asked me, *"Who hurts more when a child is hurt, the child or the parent?"* I understand that. The shadows were using me in yet another cruel and evil facet simply to get at God. That's why they never stop coming after me, and my refusal to tell before only helped their unholy cause. I wasn't doing it intentionally but I was doing it nonetheless, cooperating and never telling, and I am now so sorry for that too.

Chapter SEVEN

I am invisible, understand, simply because people refuse to see me.

Ralph Ellison

NO SAFE PLACE

My counselor says it is sad that I never found a safe place such as in the scouts or Little League. There was no safe place in my young world, or so it seemed to me. No matter where I went, the shadows were there with me, but their presence in me was invisible to those around me. My pain was invisible to them as well. I tried Little League one season, but I was so bad at it that they put me in right field, considered the easy position where that kid could not do much damage to the team. I was born without depth perception and later learned this was why I could not catch or hit a baseball. I had no way of really seeing it coming. Because of the physical defect, I was doomed to a childhood of poor athletic ability. That is until I found karate.

The other Little Leaguers didn't know either and mocked me. Kids can be naturally mean that way, and my coaches were indifferent to stopping it. Some of them even took a few shots at me as well. They probably figured it would "toughen the boy up" but all it did was create in me a hatred for playing the game. The sentiment remains with me to this day. It was a painful experience like so many others, and it was yet another chain that bound me to the manipulations of the shadows. My attempts to play baseball ended in the early days of my military enlistment, when I was laughed off the field and humiliated for the last time. I will never play the game again.

I was a Cub Scout and loved that. Later, we moved and I joined the Boy Scouts, and for a brief time, I loved that too. It was a safe place for a while but that would not last long. We had relocated to a small town, and in my scout troop there, I somehow managed to annoy the scoutmasters. They let me know it along with the fact that they did not like me. I should have already known that adults can be just as mean as kids but it still caught me off guard.

At scout camp, where it's supposed to be fun, I also felt out of place. Our scout camp was in the mountains, and I found solace sitting on a large rock with a spectacular view. Like other places I discovered, it was one of solitude where I knew that I would not bother anyone. I went there on the last day, thankful camp was about to be over, and while sitting alone there, I lost track of time. They apparently thought I had run away or was lost. A search party was organized and someone located me.

"I thought I would find you here" said one of the young adults who worked at the camp.

"Everyone is looking for you."

Oh great; unintentionally I had messed up again and I knew it. We walked back to the scout camp in silence and no one said anything. We just got into the vans and went home.

Not long after that, we moved to the city and somehow, my scout records got lost. I was told that to join a new troop, I'd have to start over as a tenderfoot and re-earn all of my merit badges. It just was not fun anymore or worth it. With that, I simply gave up on scouting as an outlet for my time since the joy was gone from it. I can't say it was anyone's fault but I'm equally unsure how I had annoyed the scoutmasters so much, or why none of them ever bothered to speak with me about it or ask if anything was wrong. I guess to them a sad, distant kid was someone else's problem.

It had been a safety net for me for a while, as no one ever touched me in the scouts. With all that did happen and my feeling uncool, unwanted, and out of place once again, the shadows had again maneuvered my life away from what was good for me. It made it easier for them to direct me further down a bad path, and the trap held me even more tightly, with one more new chain.

– Look Me in the Eyes –

As an adult, I did give clues about my past but they were very subtle. For me, making eye contact is very difficult; it has to be forced, but I can do it. I would come to find out that people still noticed and made assumptions about me and about my character because of that. We don't have a lot of information when we first meet someone, so it's human nature to fill in the gaps and guess about why they act a certain way. Sometimes, we can do unnecessary harm to others through our assumptions about them.

In my case, during the last job performance review I got before being laid off, my supervisor noted what I thought was an odd remark, and it worried me greatly. He said that one of the feedback comments he had gotten on me was that I didn't look people in the eye, even though I thought I was pretty good at covering my fear there. It was easy to figure out that the comment had come from our new department head...my new boss. It worried me instantly because we all knew that by September of that year, she was going to cut one of our positions. The comment was followed up with another one stating she felt that this indicated dishonesty and deception in me. I have never been dishonest at work; it's not part of my ethics. That may be hard to believe, but I have always had some standards, and being honest in my work is one of them.

After the layoff, when I was talking with my counselor, I discovered this trait of avoiding eye contact was a tragic result of my programming. From somewhere in the past, another memory has surfaced, and I remember being told to "Look me in the eye, boy." Today, if I am having a difficult conversation with someone, making eye contact is nearly impossible for me without a lot of forced effort from inside myself, but at the same time, I am a good listener. I didn't notice the eye contact issue until the comment came up in my performance review. It was another hidden snare on me and one cleverly designed by the shadows to hurt me again, which it did when I lost my job later that year.

How much of a role that played in the decision to cut me from the workforce that last time, or times before, I simply don't know. I'm working on it now, and it's not as hard to do most of the time. I also made a point of telling the director that I was an abuse survivor. I told her that no one should ever make such uninformed comments about others like that, as there may be a really good reason for their behavior. I didn't give any of the details, but she got the message, and her apology was sincere.

Thinking on it later, I don't feel that she intended any unkindness by the comment, but during my review, I received it that way regardless. In an odd way it was a blessing, as it was a beginning for me in understanding that I have a problem with this. It got me to thinking how important it is to not let my own first impressions about others allow me to judge them wrongfully. I'm no different from anyone in that regard, and now I have a better understanding of the impact my words can have on people. I will try harder to be kinder and less hurtful toward others in the future. It has taught me that God does work in interesting ways within us and through us. This is a good start for me, and I'm a better person through His efforts. After years of self-imposed silence, it was sheer desperation that finally brought me to a point where I had to tell someone. I had been badly hurt and confused long enough, and had reached a breaking point. The job layoff finally put me there. That is where God found me. When He did, I was finally ready for His work to begin.

Chapter EIGHT

You may be deceived if you trust too much, but you will live in torment if you don't trust enough.
Frank H. Crane

REDEEMED

I have a feeling inside now that my prayers are finally about to be answered. There were so many years of praying too, but now I am seeing a light. This angel working with me now is actually my second counselor. After two years of painful on and off visits with my first one, I thought I was over all of it, that I could put it all aside and move on into a normal life. I really did. Then I lost my job and the old feelings came flying back into my thoughts. The shadows started to whisper to me in the darkness, *"Loser; there is really only one thing you've ever been good for, and that was as a kid. You're not good for anything now."*

It is sad to say, but once again I started to believe them. After my visits to the first counselor stopped, it seemed like the shadows had been on an extended absence, and I started to think they were finally gone. It was the longest they had ever been absent from my dreams, but they returned again with a vengeance to take advantage of my job loss. I guess they were mad that I started down this road to healing. I don't really care now what they think.

– First Steps to Healing –

I've intentionally chosen Christian counselors because I still have some small measure of hope that God has not given up on me. I figure that any success must come from Him and through my counselors. Each has helped me sort this out from a different perspective. The first got me past one of the toughest places of all, to where I could finally start talking. She was close to my mom's age, and I was pretty sure when I first walked into her office that she would be shocked, maybe even disgusted by me. I was afraid, as this was getting into bad territory and after all, how could you ever talk to someone like your mom about "that"?

However, she had this disarming manner, like my current counselor. I started to trust her almost immediately in my first session. This stuff didn't make her think I was weird at all, because she knew it happens even to boys. Unfazed by and nonjudgmental about anything I said, she helped me to start to tear down barriers of fear behind which I have hidden for too many years. Together, we sorted things out *intellectually,* and that got me to a point where I could truly understand that every story has a beginning, middle, and an end, as she told me. She also pointed out that for me, all of the physical events ended in reality long ago, and now they needed to end in my mind too. I wanted that so much.

Because of her sessions, when I see something on television or in the movies now that triggers a fear–memory, I can more easily deal with it right then even if I don't know exactly why I reacted with fear, which is sometimes the case. She taught me, too, that as an adult, I have reasoning, which a child doesn't have. When you are little and older people tell you things about yourself, or tell you to do something, when they say you have flaws or tell you all of the bad things are *your* fault…you believe it. For a kid, it's that simple. If an adult says it, it must be true. With counseling, I started to see that for what it was, nothing but lies.

Finally, she taught me to understand that because of experiences, my mind has a hair-trigger defense mechanism and maybe it always will. At least now that I know it's there, I can better control it too. At times in the past, my hair-trigger sadly caused me to react inappropriately, becoming upset over stupid things. Later, I would stress and then feel bad because the damage was done. For me, not knowing what actually flipped the switch would make me afraid of when it would happen again. I knew well that more anger would lead to more trouble for me, as it always had. I still do not yet have complete control in recognizing when the switch is about to be flipped, but I am better at it. So that, too, is coming to an end.

My counselors have helped me to deal with different areas of my confusion in different ways. They both knew (or know, as in the case of my current counselor) what I needed to do to be set free. Many times before, I have tried to rid myself of this sadness on my own. It simply has not worked. My efforts always failed no matter how hard I worked at it. Maybe I failed because I'm not a professional in the psychology of these things. I really don't know. Regardless, I see this as my last hope.

(I figured out later that there was no way I could win by myself because I was trying to beat sin without believing God would want

to help me with that. That is part of the truth Jesus speaks about. Without Him, we cannot win that fight. When I wrote the passages above, I still did not really understand that idea, but I do now.)

– The Holy Spirit's Hand –

My second counselor has taken me down a more *spiritual* road. We are still walking that path as I write this. I started to see her because even though I had grown enough to deal with last summer's final nightmare, getting laid off again triggered something, as I said. The shadows returned and their whispers started once more in my dreams. God saw to it that the lady who was to become my second counselor would visit our church. I heard her talking about her own experiences, and it moved me. She was telling someone about her own deep look at the spiritual side of things and how that really pulled her to safety. She noted that she worked with abuse survivors. Something clicked in my mind, and hesitantly, I approached her about the abuse topic. I was trying to be ever so casual in my manner. It was not quite as pathetic as the old *"I have this friend who…"* tactic but almost as obvious. I am practiced at hiding it, but in talking to her I hoped she would pick up on that. She spotted me right away and knew I was reaching out. Somehow she asked the right questions, starting with:

"So, when were you abused?"

It was the direct approach, and it caught me totally off guard, to say the least. I still had some shielding up, but she saw through that easily enough too. I asked how she knew that. She said, *"I can see it in your eyes."*

I was stunned. No one had ever said that to me before, never seen what my eyes were hiding. With her, my disguise did not work. We went to one of the meeting rooms and talked, and I liked her imme-diately. She told me to go home and pray on it, then call her. So I did. Nervous and kind of angry in approaching that prayer, I told the Spirit in an annoyed tone, *"If you promise it will work this time, I promise to do what the counselor says and go where you lead me."*

See, this was not the first time I had prayed on it, and I even won-dered if I was being tricked again, which is where my frustration came from. In truth, I knew we can't take on God in anger and win, but really, I had written myself off and believed He had written me off as well. So I figured I would just try to cut myself a deal with the Creator of the Universe and see where it led no matter what the tone. The Spirit did answer me in that moment, yet there was no anger pro-jected back at me for my attitude in His response. It was just a calm reply and a single, powerful, word that showed up huge in my mind, like a giant billboard. He said:

"Agreed."

At the same time, I clearly heard that answer audibly. Perhaps the Spirit knew I needed both to be convinced. Well it worked, and I got my bargain. I stood there thinking; *What did I just do?* Yet quickly, I decided that wherever this was going to lead, it had to be better than where I was at. So it was with that step I began the second leg of my healing journey, just after the start of the New Year, 2011.

While my first counselor was also a Christian, my new one takes a different and more prayerful God–strong approach to dealing with me. She is a charismatic believer, and I had no idea who these people were, but knew that's what I needed even if I wasn't sure exactly why. She knows where the switches are and can get me to crying as part of the release process. Normally, I really hate losing control like that, and I equally don't like being way out of my comfort zone, but I have to admit that the tears bring relief now, and I don't have to cry alone anymore.

For some reason, I'm not bothered that she can do this. I'm actually cool with her using her "Jedi powers" on me because I still have work to do. I'll need her help to do it. I don't understand everything that she asks me to do, but know it's for the best. God chose the right path for me whether I find it comfortable or not. She tells me too that God collects my tears. He must have gallons by now.

These sessions are like stumbling over the rocky path of learning to live with this great sadness. I've referred to it that way in my mind for many years, long before the book called *The Shack* came out, where the author uses that term. When I read it, I fully related to descriptions of the great sadness in the story even though the main character, Mac, had a different source of his pain. Both counselors have taught me that the sadness I've lived with is nothing but left-over waste from the abuse, imprinted on my mind and imposed on my body during my early life. Recognizing that fact sounds simple enough, but it gets darn difficult when one has spent as much time as I have denying that it all happened. That just doesn't work anymore. I am tired of trying and never getting anywhere, and tired of only being able to remember my life that way. So here I am on a new path.

My counselor says I have to be able to say it out loud. I can say, "I was abused." Maybe not to everyone and certainly not everywhere, but now I can say that sometimes. I will *not* say the M-word—molested. I hate that word. I anguish over and despise the hurt and confusion that it stirs inside of me. It's like a brand someone put on me, and I can't tear it off or make it go away no matter what. Even writing it now makes me cry. It has not found a safe place in my vocabulary, and I think it much too often. When I can change what thinking or saying that word does to me emotionally, it'll be a good thing, but I'm not there yet.

I cannot explain why, but perhaps saying that much is a start, somehow. One thing is clear, my counselor is not going to let me get away with saying, *"Let's just skip this step or that part of the process or whatever it's called...and move right along to something less difficult and painful."* I've tried, too, but she just doesn't pay any mind to that comment. She is as tough as anyone I've ever met yet so very gently pushy in a kind way. I have to work on it, much as I don't want to. She knows what she is doing, and I trust her fully. I have to trust someone to get this evil out of me. I promised the Spirit that I would, too.

To look at her, you would not guess she's endured terrible abuses in her own past, nor would you guess the tremendous strength she has inside. For that reason, I think she can read me like a book. I'm cool with her being able to see me more clearly then I can see myself. That makes it easy for me to trust her. It's like talking to God since I understand now that He already knows everything, and I kind of figure she does too, somehow.

Like my first counselor, she does not judge me no matter what comes spilling out. Even so, I still hesitate to tell her details that I've not yet sorted out or wonder if maybe some are not real. I just don't know how to look at it realistically.

– The Defeat of Shame, Guilt, and Fear –

My counselor has taught me about the cycle of shame, guilt and fear. I wish so much that I had understood the cycle when I was a kid. It's a fairly simple concept but explains so much about how people deal with things like abuse. Essentially, *shame* kept me feeling *guilty* about things, and that led to a *fear* of being rejected by my family, by God, and by anyone who discovered this secret. I let fear control me, and it was fear that kept me from getting the help I needed. Fear kept me away from God. As a kid, I gave the game controller for my life to the shadows, who delighted in using it against me in the evil game they had invented for me.

I've started to break that cycle, but only because I finally figured out that I had to reach out to someone to do it. I do not feel shame anymore through seeing things for what they were. It is not the kid's fault; it's the fault of the abusers, and ultimately, it is the fault of the enemy. I don't feel guilt either because it's dawned on me that God already knows everything. He has already forgiven me, not written me off or erased me from history. I am here, and I am healing now in Him. Having broken the chains of shame and fear, I've put the controller for my life in God's hands.

Even so, the shadows still try to tell me this is not going to work out well but I know differently. With God in control, we have given the shadows an eviction notice from my soul. Their time is limited.

Inside of me, there is a very large bundle of anger that is boxed up somewhere. I have seen a small part of it, but right now, I really do not want to look at that anymore or let it out, and I told my counselor this. What I want is to go after these shadows. That's not an option for me just by myself, either, but payback time for all of this hurt is coming soon. STUPID SHADOWS! Who were you to do this to me? Maybe I can't come to your spirit dimension and hurt you directly but guess what…God can! I cut my deal with the Spirit, and He can come after you no matter where you are hiding inside of me or in this world. Are you listening? You'd better be, and you'd better be afraid too. The angel knows someone who can see you in your dark world and take you on directly, too, so you have lost already. In my world, I can try to stop you from infecting others with your evil, and I will. I am pretty sure God's going to show me how to do that and how to fight you! Yeah, I'm getting close to finding more of my anger, and I'm going to use it in the right way to fight you because God will show me how.

–

I had to pause as writing the last few sentences took a lot out of me. I have not tapped into any part of my anger before and had to walk away from this for a day to catch my breath. More relaxed now, I recognize that I have to figure out how to find the box of anger inside and express it in the right or beneficial way. This is something I do not want to do, but have to. My counselor can help me do that, and my wife's love, too, will give me the strength. God is here, and He's given me a great pastor whom I can turn to as well.

I have to be angry with those who molested me. I have a right to be angry with them. That's sad, because I suspect that every one of them was molested too. It's a terrible cycle, but not everyone who was molested becomes a predator despite what people assume about that. That is just another label people who don't understand this experience put on survivors. What I did before finding this path was choose to turn the blame inward, where it turned into depression and hurt me more. I don't know why some choose one path and others another, or why someone who feels this pain can inflict it on others. It's the same thing as the idea that all boys who are beaten grow up to beat their own wives and children. Right now, I must place blame where it belongs. Having sorted out at least this much, when I see children these days, I say, *"Keep them safe, Lord"* quietly to myself. It is my prayer that He does, because I know well what happens when the alternative takes over.

My counselor angel says that when I get through all of this, I'll be able to help others by testifying. She says I'll find a blessing in all of this through that, and my pastor said the same thing. My response was to say there's no way can I see that happening. Me testifying? You have got to be kidding. She just smiled kindly and ignored my response. I thought to myself; *How could I even find the words?*

(Ultimately, I would not have to worry about finding the right words; the Spirit would provide them. I just didn't know it when I wrote the thoughts above.)

Chapter NINE

A sad soul can kill you quicker, far quicker than a germ.

John Steinbeck

THE ANGER BOX: A TURNING POINT

The fact is I have yet to get really angry about the abuse or those involved. They helped to create this sad soul inside me but it didn't kill me. I am still here and fighting back now. Long ago, I convinced myself that because I am not sin-free and for that reason alone, I cannot say *anything* at all about the activities of others, even those they inflicted on me. Through that reasoning, the sadness was able to find another claw-hold in my heart and a way to live on inside.

At school and later at work, there were times people would not even want to be around me because of my edgy personality. In my mind, I frequently storyboarded small events into mountainous catastrophes far worse than they actually were. I got very good at storyboarding. That is the ability to draw in our mind a whole series of events and add things that were not intended or even real to turn something totally upside down and distort reality. It's taking things way out of context, and they become something far more negative or hurtful than what actually happened. I am still good at doing that.

For example, a rude brush-off could easily become a conspiracy in my mind. In turn, this would manifest itself in a confrontation or snarky comment from me to another student, professor, or coworker, making things even worse. In the end, people sometimes decided they could not understand me or just didn't want me around, and who could blame them? Well, I did blame them. Then I blamed myself, and it would all just get worse.

The result was that I became more isolated and lonely. Accordingly, my time in graduate school was one of the saddest and most difficult periods of my life. Not all of it was because of me either. Some people are just cruel or indifferent for whatever reason, but looking back at it now and seeing what I was like at times, I can easily understand why some people shunned me.

No one can blame people for not wanting to be around an angry young man. I get that, but it's sad nonetheless that no one ever asked me why I was angry. Not once. Truly, how can people simply not see when others are hurting or discard them like that? In saying this, it does make me wonder how many times I have done the same thing to others as well and also failed to see when *they* were in pain. Had anyone ever asked, I'm not sure I could have even identified a single cause of my attitude at the time because I had blocked out so much in my mind. All of this storyboarding and blame game is something I have to sort out with my counselor, as I have never understood it or its source.

In addition to everything else, my stepfather had died just before I started graduate school. He was a true role model for me growing up and was now gone. Sadly, shame, guilt and fear kept me from telling him about the things that had happened, or all of this could have ended years before. But I wasn't able to do that, and now he was gone. Also, I only ended up going to graduate school because the military had cut its active duty forces after the Gulf War. Along with many other young people, I got the boot back into the civilian world, and for me, it was another sign of rejection. I was totally sure God would keep me in the service, which is what I wanted most. Being pushed out like that made it feel like God had left me too.

All of it was, of course, just another set of lies I bought into from the enemy, as I had no clue then about such things. To make matters worse, my family thought my going to graduate school was a stupid choice and I got that message loud and clear. So the collective impact of these events, plus the ever-present "sadness" combined in a perfect storm inside of me. That storm would push my heart deeper into a tired desperation and outlook on life. I considered suicide.

In that moment, it was very easy to do, standing on the fifth floor open balcony of my school's building, looking down at the pavement below. I kept thinking this would be so easy and then there would be no more hurt of any kind. A dark voice whispered in my ear that no one would miss me, hell they didn't even like me around there, the voice said. That was true enough to some degree, but not totally. A stronger voice told me I *would* be missed, that I *did* have friends and that my family *did* love me even if I didn't see it all at the moment. The second voice won the argument. It had to have been an angel I think. They're the messengers of God and that message got through. Though I didn't fully understand or agree at the time, I knew it was speaking the real truth. I stepped away from the railing, but there would be one more challenge in that direction before I was able to destroy such thoughts for good. I now know that my time here is up only when God says so, not me, and thoughts of suicide are not an issue anymore.

Thanks to the angel speaking one lonely night on that balcony, I came to realize something very important. I had gotten a great deal of compassion from several people at school. I had two good student friends, one who was also a Christian. I also had one Christian professor. They all clearly cared about me in those days, and I understand that now with grateful appreciation. Later we had a visitor to our class, a Navajo man who also touched my soul with much-needed kindness. He quietly whispered relief into my ear one evening before he left our student group for good. Before walking away from the dinner table, he bent over and told me softly:

"It is time to let go of those who have passed on."

This provided a real voice, from someone who had finally seen inside me and saw the hurt there. It was an answer to my prayers. After nearly three years of grieving the loss of my stepfather, I understood at once that he was right. The process of letting go of my stepfather started that night. I hope that God blesses him forever for his kindness. He gave that gift to me at a time when it seemed most others were totally indifferent to my pain. The other students at the table asked what he had said to me, as I'm sure I looked stunned, but I could not tell them what he had said and just mumbled something. I have no idea what I said, but something powerful had been stirred inside of me.

His compassion, along with my friend's kindness and that from the professor, all helped me start the process of figuring out where my anger and hurt came from. It was a start, but unfortunately the answers I needed were still years away yet. Along that path, darkness waited before I would find the light.

Chapter TEN

I have been driven many times upon my knees by
the overwhelming conviction that I had nowhere
else to go. My own wisdom, and that of all about
me, seemed insufficient for that day.

Abraham Lincoln

FINDING ANGER

I find myself on my knees a lot during this process. More than once,
people who know about this have said I need to deal with the anger.
I don't feel angry like they say I should be able to feel it. I'm probably
just denying that it's there. Deep inside, I really don't know *how* to
do it. I don't know how to get angry in the right way, or as my pastor
says, the beneficial way. What is that? How do I start? I feel like if I
give in to anger then I'll be giving in to hate. This path is hard, like
the others, and it hurts just as much even if it is supposed to help me.

Almost everyone I've told about the sadness says I need to get
angry about what happened to me and those who did it. I have done
that, somewhat, but not openly or really expressed it out loud. Inside,
I'm still numb about this. The ever-present question in my mind is
this: *How can I get angry with people when I don't even know who*

they are or were? I get that I should be angry at what they did and the choices they made to do it, but what I really want is to be forgiving, and my counselor says forgiveness does not mean we cannot be angry, yet how to make that combination work is totally unclear to me. This is one more of the many rotten emotions that keep rising up out of this whole thing. I am conflicted and confused by all of it.

Still, if that's the direction I'm led, it's time to face this too, even if I don't want to. For the moment, others say they'll be angry for me until I learn to let it out. I love them so much for that and for so many other things. My counselor is with me too, feeling what I will not yet let myself feel. I fear this, but I've already learned from her how to start sorting all of it out and how to put it into the right perspective.

At the start, I told my counselor that I do not know who the people were who molested me. She said, *"Sure you do."*

"No, I don't; they were strangers," I told her.

I can't even see their faces in my mind; the shadows hide them, so how am I to know who they were? They hid themselves too. Does that mean if I look deep enough into the memories I'll see their faces and remember their names? Or worse, remember even more of the stuff that I would rather forget? Then what?

If I recognize them, my counselor says we could go after them because they could still be hurting kids. She says we could stop them and prevent some other kid from having to live through this nightmare. It has thus become my obligation, and that in itself is yet another hurt, as this has now become *my responsibility* to do something no matter how difficult. It is a powerful argument for me, yet knowing this does not make it any easier to go in that direction. It makes me feel like it will be my fault if I don't try and my fault if someone else gets hurt. That doesn't seem fair, either, but who said life is fair? If I can stop others from being hurt, well, that is reason enough alone to do it, so I'll pray and take God's direction.

The second challenge for me is this. My counselor tells me getting angry will help me, too. Really? I am not sure how anger will help at all, but I trust her fully, so maybe this will take me one more step closer to being totally free of the sadness. Just like the Oprah show helped me, maybe writing all of this will help someone else seek out a good counselor and start to heal too. It does seem to me like there are a lot of steps I have to take to get through this. There are rules I have to follow if I want to get right with God, even if I don't understand it all or don't have a clue as to how these rules apply to me.

I'm told there are "subconscious contracts" with evil in me, contracts that are part of my story. And I'm told I have to break them, but how? So what happens if I trip up in the future by being unfair or mean to someone? Have I then signed yet another contract of some kind with evil that will apply to my family later? I really don't get how a contract with evil was set up with me at age five or six, when I could not possibly agree to it, or why what something some ancestor did should be taken out on me. Tell me God, please, or is asking this going to get me in trouble too?

At times, it feels like it's all too much to sort out. My ever-present child side says that it's just not fair. Another question I have is why God doesn't simply free me now. It seems like there are a lot of questions to ask still, so I will try to do that and listen for the answers.

In response, again, my counselor asked me this: If we don't know what sorrow is, how can we really understand the joy of having a true relationship with God? I know what sorrow is, for crying out loud. I've lived with it for decades; isn't that enough already? Guess this means I'm still angry with God and really do not want to be. We cannot understand the whole essence of God. If He's everything I'm told He is, then I am in for some incredible joy. It's already starting and that helps, because knowing that much somehow pulls me back into a place where I see that I'm not really angry with Him. Perhaps I'm just angry at still feeling confused.

God is, well, God. I'll never have a better friend who loves me more. He did not have to rescue me, but He chose to. For that reason, I have to keep going forward as much as this whole thing bites. God is telling me to keep going and he has all the time and patience of creation to walk slowly with me. So all right, I am willing to trust once more. I thank God that He has given me so many friends now who know I'm working on this. They are people to lean on. Having them in my life makes it possible, as I have never been able to get this far on my own.

Time to move on and look at this anger thing. As a starting point of reference, I have to complain about my experience with anger in the past. Why? Because that is what's causing me to hesitate and it explains why I don't want to find the anger inside. Anger has never been good for me. People also say they can see anger in my fifth grade school picture, but I don't see it. We had moved to a new state and I was around ten years old. My aunt says I would storm around like a kid who was mad at the whole world. I remember that very well. That feeling of being absolutely furious at stupid things like the neighbor kid cutting through our yard. I see that now for what it was. It was not just silly behavior; it was lashing out. Yet none of the adults in my life were interested in helping me deal with it. It is possible they just thought it was the result of my parents' divorce and having moved to a new state. Maybe the adults in my family had tried too, and I just didn't notice or don't remember their efforts now.

Even so, some relatives tell me now they thought it was all *funny*. Why did no one ask or look further into what was really going on in my mind? How's an eleven-year-old supposed to sort that out since they don't have the mental or emotional ability yet to do so? Kids are supposed to be innocent. I wasn't. That was stolen from me even though I didn't know it. All I know was that I hurt inside and I had no words for it.

So it was the anger that continued to live in me as a teenager and into adulthood. My expressions of it, either through outbursts or pouting in those years, never did me any good. If I got angry with adults who were using me as a little kid, it didn't work out well either. I was threatened more than once with getting beaten if I didn't comply, and even hit sometimes, regardless. A kid can't consent anyway; a kid can only comply. To me, cooperating equaled being good, good for something, but it was still coupled with fear. I see clearly now that the idea of being "good for something" was another false identity, another lie from the shadows that was part of a twisted game they wanted to play out on me.

Thinking about it now, I can write down a list of events throughout my life that stung like a nest of hornets, which can still stir up the anger inside me. Events like when professors or other students would mock me in class and around school. That made me angry. I can get angry at times when employers treated me unfairly and held me to a higher standard than they held themselves to. I can get angry at people at work who did far less than I and got away with it for years, yet it was me chosen for the last layoff and not one of them. It all makes me angry, but the truth is everyone is treated unfairly at some time.

That's life and it bites sometimes. Just deal with it son. My list, like anyone else, could go on for pages, but the point is made.

So it is that I have to learn now to see anger differently. More importantly, to find it in me and let it go. I'm trying hard to remember that God will deal with all of the unfairness, so we don't have to worry about it anymore. Well, that one is a tough pill to take and buy into. Regardless, I really do want that idea to sink into my heart, to become part of my thoughts inside. It will release me from all the anger described from my past. Tough or not, it is the only path worth taking now.

As for the abuse, I know there is anger deep inside of me about how people could do any of that to a kid, whether it was verbal, physical, emotional or sexual. All of my anger about it hides in the same box. It's there along with the anger I'm holding onto toward those who should have protected me, those who didn't notice or ask questions. Every kid should have a real sense of being valued or feeling safe. A kid should be able to trust someone, and adults are supposed to give them that. My thinking got messed up early, and I am angry with that too. It's all sitting in that box somewhere deep inside. I need to find a way to drill down to it and let it go, but I do not really want to go there.

Here's the next stumbling block I put into my own path. I tell myself that *you* didn't communicate, ever. *You* are the one who chose to keep it all a secret. I did kind of try with the psychologist at college, but never trusted him enough to really go there because in my mind, it was my fault. So my thinking again puts the blame back onto me. Those lies that I came to believe as a small child and teenager had chained me to a wall of self-blame. That *was* true then about my thinking, but it is starting to fade in me, being replaced by a truth that is real.

Looking hard at my life, I find now that there were always people around me who cared, even if they could not stop the unfairness or abuse. It is clear to me now that had they known, they would have stopped it. Had I not fallen into the trap of accepting false identities and ungodly beliefs about myself, many of those times would have been different. The lies imprinted in my thinking were all from the shadows and are yet another facet of their cruelty. Understanding that now, I ask myself another question. Should the anger be directed at the acts of abuse and unfairness, or at the people who did them, or both? I think the right answer is both in some proper measure. My counselor keeps saying I can still be forgiving but that to get there fully, I have to be angry first.

– Open the Door –

With that box of anger so well hidden in my mind, I have to figure out how to find it. That's the tough part because there were points in my life when I tried to find it and turn the anger off but instead it focused inward and turned on me.

I once read somewhere that anger turned inward becomes depression. That makes total sense to me, as it has been my experience on a regular basis. It would routinely come around to shake my understanding of myself, my world, and thus weaken the foundations of anything I felt like I had accomplished or done well. That little whisper in the back of my mind kept saying, *"You were not made for anything good."* My worst episodes of depression were as a college student. I tried to talk to one of the psychologists at school., At the end of our last session, he just said, *"You have a problem with authority figures son."*

Little did he know. I did tell him at our first meeting that I didn't want to talk about sex issues, so he never took his questions in that direction. At the time I was talking to him, I was also grieving the loss of my stepfather, and perhaps he thought that was the root of my problems. It seems to me now that my comment about "no sex issues" should have been a huge red flag to focus on in our sessions. How can a university psychologist, trained to work with young people, not see when a student is purposefully dodging a hurtful issue? As a result, the counseling I sought at school never helped because it never got into the real problem, the abuse in my past. I walked away from it still feeling empty.

As to that authority figure thing, I did have a problem with some professors. One time, sitting outside of a professor's office, I heard her and a student talking about scholarship awards. My name came up on their list and the professor glibly said, *"We'll give it to him if he agrees to get a lobotomy."* They both had a good laugh, not knowing I was sitting right outside the door. They didn't know I was there, but I then knew exactly how they really felt about me. That told me I'd blown it again, and sadly, I had thought this other student was my friend, too.

My sense of failure was further solidified when a guest professor pulled me aside one day. He recommended that I find another major as, in his view, my work showed no gift at all. He once told me coldly during class, *"I know you think you're too old to start over but you're not, and you really have no talent for this."*

It was one of the few times he had ever spoken directly to me, even though I had just as much right to seek his help as anyone else in class. So there it was, bam! Trashed and devastated again. Looking at it now, with the help of God and my counselor, I see there were others who spoke favor over me, but in my world, I had learned to let the negative words have a stronger hold than the positive ones. Again, I see the enemy at work, using our own weaknesses to let us dig that hole even deeper.

Maybe all of this sounds petty and like whining, but my life has been full of episodes like it and I could go on and on. I feel like I've had more than my share, but who doesn't feel that way at times? Whether that is true or not, I'm sure the shadows were behind things as they looked for ways to stab at my soul and make me regret even being born. These almost daily moments of hurt further set me up to become an easy target for the enemy's schemes. Collectively, these events led me to a balcony railing five floors above some concrete stairs to consider that final option. Staring down at the pavement, my thoughts were of how easy it would be to just leave. Simply by climbing over and letting go, I could leave school, leave the world and leave the hurt behind. Obviously, I did not listen to that voice of evil telling me to just do it, but I continued to live in a state of accepting ungodly beliefs about myself, all the same. To me, I had no value. I was the leftover shell of some kid used up years ago and nothing more.

– A Light in the Darkness –

The good news is that I never stopped praying to God every night to help me, and He did. I'm not really even sure why I prayed, to be honest, as my sense of self was one of having been written off but there you go, it's God at work again. He provided more help too. Three other professors saved me in those days, along with my two friends. One professor talked me out of dropping out. She said I *did* have a talent that she could see, even if no one else did (including me). She convinced me to give it one more semester, which I did, and ultimately, I got my degree…thanks to her. One other professor, who was my advisor, told me the guest teacher always picked a student to trash and that I should not pay any attention to him. Why, I asked? After all, that guy was a star in the field so his opinion should say it all, right? It doesn't, my advisor told me, as that man had no right to say that and predict some kid's future. My advisor told me he had done that once to a kid, and now that former student was the head of a major firm in the profession.

"I'll never play God with a kid's life again," he said. *"And don't let him play God with your life Sean."*

I would keep going.

The last of my saving professors was one of my toughest, but he was also a Christian. He simply reminded me one day that I was a child of God, God's creation, and that I had just as much right to seek my dreams as anyone else. We just talked a lot. Had I known how to say what was really at the heart of my sadness, I could have talked to him, but in those days, I was still in denial, still letting the shadows convince me that I was flawed beyond repair, and still totally convinced that if I said anything about "that" to anyone, they would reject me. The shadows had taught me that it was impossible for me to change. I know now that it was all a lie, a false and ungodly belief, and I'm not buying into it anymore. While it no longer defines me, I really wish I had learned all of this about myself a whole lot sooner.

I am grateful God sent an angel to pull me away from that railing at school with loving words to whisper hope into one ear while the shadows were in my other ear saying I was worthless and should jump. I am grateful God also sent the Navajo man whose quiet advice helped me to move on from mourning my stepdad's passing. As for my two friends, the ones who had stuck by me even when I was a difficult person to be around, I am certain they too were God sent. For them, I am grateful, too, and have so much love for God for placing all of them into my life during those sad days. It would take some years yet for me to see that for myself, to realize what I had in those days and what my relationship with God really was then and now. What they gave me was something to hold onto, a connection with the Creator that I didn't know I had yet was fully established even then. Through it all, I kept praying because my friends made sure I did not lose all hope, and I think it was the start of my being set free through this process. It would still be a long time before I would find my counselor, but I'm here now.

The angry sadness inside remained. After school, bad things happened at work that were the result of my not expressing it well. A few years ago, I finally had enough of myself and decided to really change something inside. I had to seek out the source of my problems to get off of my destructive path. My problems were not my coworkers' fault, nor were they even really my fault entirely. They came from the programming and false beliefs that were well entrenched in my subconscious. I didn't know they were there, but knew something about me had to change, and I was the only one who could make it happen or at least start the process.

Once I started to see the false beliefs clearly through counseling and self-assessment, I was able to start dealing with them effectively, one by one. People said they noticed a change in me for the better. It was not enough to save me from being laid off again, but it was enough to give me strength to work through unemployment now without falling back into my depression. My new employer, whoever they will be, will get a much better me and things are really going to work out well for both of us.

Chapter ELEVEN

Although the world is full of suffering, it is also full of overcoming it.

Helen Keller

YOU HAVE TO GO NOW!

Helen Keller was right. I know that neither my counselor (or the Holy Spirit) would be asking me to find and face the anger if it was not going to lead to something better. My course is now clear. I have to look inside myself to find that box of anger, open it, and let all of that go. This all started by my bargaining once again with God. I told Him I would do this because of my promise to follow His direction, but I would have to do this in my own way and in my own time. There, the challenge was out and perhaps God would let me off the hook this time. Nope. Instead, He gently used my own words to prompt me onward.

"That's OK if you do this in your own way; I do things in my own way too. It's how I made you. Argue all you want, but I have all eternity to wait you out" was the reply to my challenge.

Man, God wins the debate again, and gives better than He gets from me. Yet here I was trying to outwit the Creator of the Universe, so what did I expect? I kind of felt like I'd been tricked into doing this but that wasn't at all true, of course. God doesn't operate that way. Instead, He sends us on the right path whether we know it or not. The Spirit was right, and I knew it. I was trumped and the only way out was to move forward. With that, I sat down on the back step and considered how to take on this anger thing. I started to understand there was no right or wrong way to do it. People can find that source of pain with God's help when the answer is buried in our subconscious somewhere. To find it, we have to get past the roadblocks we set up as excuses for ignoring it and that's not easy. Ignoring all of this never did me any good in the past, so I had to face it now.

There is no right answer on this test, either, and no way to fail unless you don't do it at all. I mention this so that anyone reading my words will know that God leads us to the safe path even if it's to be a difficult one. You have God's word on that; scripture says so. He will answer your cry for help. For me the problem was how could I find and tap into the anger since it was hidden deep inside in that box, buried far back somewhere in my mind. Regardless, I had promised God that I would try. Lest I forget, the Spirit reminded me about that, too, with simple words:

"You promised."

Wow! Those words hit home in a big way. I *had* promised. He knew it, and I did too. My friends tell me this is called conviction of the Holy Spirit, but it is not the same as condemnation. The Spirit was not condemning me, only reminding me out of love. I think of it as spiritual parenting, and I'll take that. I had promised, and I hope to never again forget that.

So with me sitting there and thinking on this problem that day, my beautiful wife's words echoed in my mind once again. She had once said that she would be angry *for me* till I discovered a way to be angry for myself. Sitting there, I realized she did not deserve to bear this burden anymore, and in fact, I had no right to place it on to her shoulders in the first place. She already held too much of this hurt for me, and it was time for me to pick up the ball. I had to search my own mind and find it, but how?

I sat there and remained numb toward the abuse and nothing more, even after my bargain with God a moment before. Sitting on the back step in the warmth of the early morning sun, this particular puzzle continued to totally stump me. All right, I thought, I had tried and was about to give up. Then I hit on the answer. This task needed to be reverse engineered. I would take the things in my life *today* that made me angry and work them backward to the ultimate source of my pain, the shadows. I got a pad of paper and a pen and started to write "I am angry at…" followed by a page-long list of junk that hurt me, annoyed me, and fueled anger in my present life, even the little and silly things. It all went down on the pad, and with that the game began.

The first thing I wrote was that I was angry about having to be angry. Yep, I really was ticked off about having to do any of this, and that started it. I continued to write a page-long list of things at which I was angry…such as how my wife and myself had been treated unfairly at work, some of the things I've already described, and others I have not yet talked about. The list kept growing.

This started to prepare me to take that first step. It is Good Friday, the same day that our Lord had to bear the agonizing sins of the world on the cross. He took them all from the past, present, and future…

including mine, as the Spirit quietly reminded me in that moment, too. I knew that this step, for me, would not bring anything close to the pain Christ had suffered, but it would bring pain enough, so still, I hesitated.

Somewhere in my distant memory, I recalled looking down into an abandoned well as a little kid. It felt like I was standing once again. That well was nothing more than a round hole cut into the earth and its shaft led into darkness. I could not see the bottom. This time, the well was inside my head but clear enough, and this time, I had to jump on down into that hole. I just stood there, ready, at the edge of the pit, trying to take the first step. The still frightened six-year-old innocent in my memories begged me not to do it, and I was arguing with myself.

"It will hurt us, we gotta hide again," he pleaded.

I told the frightened child inside, *"I am going to free you now; stay here with the Spirit. You will be safe, but I have to go."*

"Well?" the Spirit gently pushed. *"You must go now."*

"Yeah I know, just give me a second," I thought back.

Pushy, I thought too. Of course the Spirit was right, as I had promised Him, my counselor, and my sweet wife that I would do this. The list of today's angers had soured my mood enough to be ready for that well and whatever it held. I was very ready. In that moment, I remembered when I told my counselor that someday, I wanted to go to the world where "it" lived. To look it straight in the eyes and make it pay. At that time in my process, I had briefly felt powerful enough to do that. It was a foolish thought because I was not ready then. I sure didn't feel ready now, either, but as they say, a promise is a promise. As they also say, be careful what you wish for. At least I fully knew I would not face this alone.

I decided that I could not do this outside; maybe just another stalling tactic. So I went back in the house with all of this in mind and put the dog out, as I didn't want her to see or feel my anger. I had what I needed. My counselor had suggested I find a sturdy pillow and put something on it to represent all of my hurt. For that, I got a piece of scrap paper and drew the outline of the older boy who had molested me at five years old, in the shed. He was the first I remember and it was his shadow. Along with that, there was my "angry" list I'd written down, so everything was there that my counselor said to assemble for this little event. I also had a photo of me from that time and I sat there staring at it, at me. The boy inside the photo stared back at the man he had become, still pleading and afraid.

I was ready, and with that I jumped into the blackness. That leap started with me pounding the pillow lightly at first and thinking still how this was ridiculous and that it was not going to lead anywhere, but soon enough, it opened a door. In powerful waves, my fists slammed into the drawing of the predator's shadow on that pillow. I still could not see his face but that didn't matter in the darkness. In my mind, I could clearly see his outline and what he first did with his coaxing, then his threats, and then everything else. I hated it and hated him in that moment. The black shape on the paper was all I needed now; it was at last something that I could hit back at, and hit I did. I had taken that step and landed in a place of total blackness. It was real but not of this world, and here I was surrounded by it. It was like being in a cocoon where I could see nothing. How could the Holy Spirit want me in a place like this? God help me.

He would help me through every part of this process, if you can call it that, and to the end of it as well, but I didn't have time to think of that in the moment. I had at last broken through my own wall and found the source of my pain. I had found my anger box. Years of hurt, disappointment, sadness, and angry words came spilling out in a torrent that flooded the darkness along with my tears. The pounding became more deliberate and intense while I searched the black corners of my mind where the shadows had hidden for years after their torments. All of my anger had been released at once in a split second. It, too, became frighteningly real, and with that, the rage began.

The shadows were there and still hiding where I could not see them. They still mocked me, even then, challenging my strength. This time, I was not afraid and let loose with everything I could think of. I started to speak, and the words just came pouring out. I spoke truth mixed with vile expletives that should not be a part of any decent person's vocabulary. Both belonged in this empty, dark and cruel place floating out into the blackness surrounding me.

I'd found the box of anger and had opened it. I was letting loose like I didn't think I knew how. My eyes stung, but I was stronger than ever before and motivated by something I did not understand. It didn't matter; this Pandora's box was shattered and everything inside of it had been set loose. This release felt strange. I'm not proud to say this, but it also felt good. I sat there wrapped in darkness catching my breath. I didn't have to wait long.

From out of the darkness, "it" appeared and looked at me. Two hateful yellow eyes formed directly in front of me, inches from my face, and snarled silent contempt in my direction. It was trying to frighten me. There I was, face to face with evil again, right there in my own home. I stared back at it with equal intensity and with an equal measure of contempt too. I stared back without fear. What I felt in that moment looking at that thing was pure hate and anger of the kind I had feared just moments before, but now I drank it in, building my strength.

"Go away!"

I shouted that in my rage, and it said nothing. It just receded into the darkness. I had no clue how to follow but I was now chasing the lion, instead of being the one hunted.

"I will find you!"

The hunted had become the hunter, and the hunter was on the move. Who is next, I thought, shouting out into the darkness, *"Bring it on!"*

So many tears again, and I opened my eyes, but I was still in the darkness of that place. It spoke in my mind, trying to strike at me with distractions about what was happening and trying to twist what I had been taught.

"What happened to forgiveness?" Its voice mocked me from the darkness.

"Forgiveness? You will not have it," I snapped back.

"What about the little boy? You left him alone."

"He's with the Spirit, and he's safe," I shouted back. *"I'm grown up now and you will deal with me. You will not hurt me anymore."*

I fired off even more challenges into the blackness with no idea what it was that heard me. I didn't care.

"Are you so blind with evil that you cannot see who is here with me? I am a child of the Most High God and He has given me power over you!"

This time, I knew I was ready. I was angry at last, and yet it still challenged me with an unspoken presence of evil and vile taunts. That only added fuel to my fire and my rage continued.

My counselor had taught me about the Armor of God and shown me in the Bible where it was described and how I could put it on. From my martial arts training, I knew that the Samurai had eighteen pieces of armor they wore into battle. I liked the Samurai imagery. They were fearless warriors. I had mentally fused their armor with that from God, and I was wearing it all now. It was my protection in that dark realm, and I'm sure Christ was there with me, but in my rage, I did not see or look for Him. I was too furious to do that. Everyone said I had a right to be angry and I was, finally, just that. I had come to agreement with what so many had told me I had a right to get angry about and to let it out. In this darkness, I was doing just that, after years of keeping it pushed down inside. The warfare continued.

More and more, I pounded the pillow and the shape of evil that I'd laid on it. I cried and God collected my tears as I hyperventilated in between tearful pleas to Him to help me. My anger poured out into the darkness and my arms hurt but I didn't care, and the pounding continued. I have no idea how long I sat there and let lose all that was crammed into that awful box.

After that evil animal-thing slunk away into nothingness, I moved on, this time to the boy in the shed who had molested me and I confronted him. I was angry that I could not see his face, and then angry that I wanted to see it. It didn't matter. The anger, the hate, the frustration, and the blame poured out of me onto a sad, anonymous form in a shed that for all I know, is gone today, in reality. Yet it still exists in the corners of my mind, where those images have lived on from that time, tormenting me. I had avoided them, but not this day. I found it. I found him. I found hate in me as I continued.

115

"YOU...do you see what you did to me, the garbage that found its way into my life because of you? You chose to do this; you CHOSE it, to hurt and molest me. You lied to me, you tricked me, then you got mad at me because I did not want to play your game. You made me do it anyway. You introduced me to things no five-year-old should know. Will I forgive you? You'll have to wait and see! For now, I want you to feel only the hurt that you laid on my soul. You stole my innocence and that was my gift from God. It was not yours to take! You stole my sense of safety for decades. You opened the door of my soul to the shadows and let them torment me! Worst of all, you led me to believe lies that it was all I was good for. That's how others found me and used me again and again. You left me with a sense that if I did not do this, I would have no other identity at all, like I never existed. You taught me to believe God had turned on me and forgotten me! YOU did that, and I hate you for it, whoever you are!"

From there, my anger focused again on the blackness where the shadows still hid. That older boy just stood there as I turned away and challenged the shadows once more.

"YOU are ultimately responsible. I'm sure you hurt this other boy and the others who molested and abused me as well. For that, you will pay! If I could, I would walk further into your darkness and find you right now."

I did want to find them, too, these shadows, being now blinded to my prior fear by a more powerful hate and anger standing in its place. I wanted to tear out their throats so that they could no longer speak evil to a child. I wanted to tear off their limbs so that they could no longer lead another person to a hurt child, or lead a child to the evil of the abuser. I wanted to reach into their dark form and pull out whatever they had for a heart, to crush the still beating thing before their yellow evil eyes. Most of all, I wanted to make them feel every hurt I had felt, then force them into a place of eternal pain for their crimes.

After some time, and I don't know how long, my anger was finally spent and I was exhausted. The pillow was sturdy and took it all undamaged, but the shape drawing was a tangled mess. I knew there was still more anger left inside but not as much and not like it was before. The Holy Spirit let me know I had done what I needed to do for now.

He pulled me out of the darkness and into the light, to a new place and still not my home in the natural. This place was still in the spiritual world, but it was filled with beautiful daylight. There was no more darkness. I was at the base of some tree, exhausted and not wanting to fight anymore. In my exhaustion, I knew there was still one more step to go and that would not be easy either. I had to take all of that hate and anger from the darkness and lay it at the foot of the cross. Looking up, that is where I found myself, at the cross. This cross was empty but it was as real as the other things I had just experienced in the darkness. There, I had to beg God's forgiveness for my judgments in that place. I had to forgive the boy in the shed and pled God's love on him because I knew that he had not started this. It was the same with everyone else who had hurt me. I also had to ask God's forgiveness for myself, for my role and my choices later on. I had to plead for His forgiveness and for my anger at the abusers, at myself, and at Him too. More strength came into me, and I did just that, confessed and asked forgiveness.

I fell into a pile on the floor, spent but now back in my own living room and in the world that I knew. It was finished. More than that, I was at the place where I really wanted to be from the start, a place where I could start to learn what forgiveness truly is. I could now start to grow that process in my heart. Once more, God had kept his promise, and I had done the same. He had to lead me through facing my anger and my fear. Together, we had started down this new path and along it more light came into my world.

Later that day, my counselor would help me start to begin to fully understand what had happened. We had done a lot that day, the Spirit and I. It was Good Friday, and I had won, the Lamb had won. The words of "Amazing Grace" rang very true for me on that day. I had come through many dangers, toils, and snares. Grace had been with me in that place of despair, it had brought me safely through. God's mercy had led me back into the light and to a stronger connection with Him.

I still have work to do, but at least now God has rescued the little boy inside of me from years of living in terror. He is completely safe at last, and he will be safe forever. I have an image of him today, of me, sleeping soundly in the palm of God's hand, wrapped in light.

With that, I can turn around, stand up and look forward with God. This battle is just the beginning. I have no idea what is coming next or what's left to deal with, but I know very well what I have left behind.

Chapter TWELVE

All truths are easy to understand once they are discovered. The point is to discover them.

Galileo

SPIRITUAL WARFARE, INTENSIFIED

At this point, my counselor pretty much knows most of my story. I have decided not to tell my family. I see no point in putting this sadness into their lives now. I had to ask myself, to what purpose? My counselor warned me that sometimes the family members do not react well to this kind of news. Thus, I made that decision because it would change nothing and only cause pain for them and myself. I must remain silent except through my words here. For me, it would also bring up questions of when, where, who, how, etc., that are questions I don't want, or know how to answer. I could show them this, but there would still be questions and the added hurt to their lives and mine by opening this subject. They do not deserve this, to have those images in their minds to the sound of my voice. Unless the Spirit directs me otherwise, my story shall remain hidden from those I love the most. I care too much about them to offer this.

There are details from those times of things that happened I will never want to discuss, get into, or revisit. God knows it all, and I'm fine with that. I can only hope that those who know some of this about me will understand. Very few others have any clue about this part of my life besides the abusers. Those details shall stay in a new box inside my mind. Unlike the anger box, it is not hidden and God has the key. He already knows it all anyway, like I said. They no longer define me or shape the direction of my life, and that's the important thing to me now.

There were many steps my counselor and I had to take before I could meet with her friend. I'm sure each counselor has different methods, and I'm not equipped to know which work the best. Mine has had me do things weekly, like draw my life as a garden with my dreams and things I love inside the garden fence and the bad things outside of the fence. As part of that exercise, I had to place myself in the picture. I drew myself with one foot inside the fence and one on the outside, as my feeling is of being part of two worlds and not totally in one or the other at any time. She also had me write two sets of letters to people. The first telling them how what they did hurt me, followed by new letters saying I forgave them. I'm not sure I believed it when I wrote them, but it was a start.

Another step involved showing me a sketch that outlined how we get from an event of abuse to the place where we accept ungodly beliefs about ourselves. We had to walk through each step as she explained how that led to the next one. Yet another took me back into the events and forced me to look harder at them, to pull details out that I had tried to forget. In that exercise, we visualized each event from start to finish, then did it over for a total of ten times in a row. It was tough and exhausting but it taught me that I could talk about this, or at least I could start to talk. Each time it was painful, but that diminished with each telling, talking and remembering. Those things are still painful to talk about, but not like before. The sheer terror of even speaking about them is gone. My counselor says with that out of the way, the healing can begin, and I believe it. I have no idea how long healing takes, but am so glad it has finally started. The wound is washed out and that infection in my soul is gone.

Without her help, I could not have done any of this. Through it all, we talked a lot and I cried a lot. I even told her things the shadows were saying to me while we were talking. Through it all, she just knew the right steps I had to take next. Every counselor is different, I'm sure, but God gives them all the tools they need to help victims of abuse become victors. Not just survivors, but also those who thrive now, free from the chains of the past.

I only recommend that others find a Christian counselor, because through them, I am able to see now how much Jesus has done for me. If you are not a Christian and still don't understand these things, at least try it. I *know* Jesus is real and that He's gotten me this far. I will do my best to keep on holding that hand from now on.

– But Deliver Us from Evil –

Like so much of my life thus far, I now hope that my description of the rest of this doesn't sound totally absurd. It's going to for anyone who has no knowledge of the spiritual warfare talked about in scripture. To those who understand what the enemy is capable of, I believe it'll ring true. What happened next *is true* as best as I can see it. Three odd weeks later, I'm still trying to understand my new self and figure out what is next for me. Here's what I can tell you about my deliverance and the last of the horrific images I would have to see through my own eyes again. It was for my good and it would be the last time I'd ever again be fearful of being unprotected.

That battle we faced in dealing with my anger? Well, that was just a taste of what was about to come. I had to go back once more into that terrifying world of the shadows where no human should ever be. I had to go there if I was to be set free. From what I'd seen the first time, I was not looking forward to it.

There is a line in the Lord's Prayer that asks God to "deliver us from evil." He was about to do that for me, though at the time I had no idea how He would do it, or what was about to happen. It is probably a good thing I didn't really know.

As I start to write this, it has been just over three weeks since I went through the process of being delivered from the evil that lived in me, which I am about to describe in as much detail as I comfortably can. The process totally exhausted me like nothing I have experienced before in life. I wrote notes immediately after we were done, and had to set them aside right afterward. So it has taken some time for me to reflect on all of it and on who I am now. I've simply not had the energy to start talking about this before, but my strength has returned. I'm ready to begin again.

I understand now that God does answer all prayers, but in His time, not ours. On that day, I was set free as He answered all of my prayers from the years before. Collected together like some pain-filled bill, God was about to show me the debt was paid in full. Christ had already paid it on the cross, but on that day before this process began, the shadows still had a grip inside of me. That grip kept me from understanding grace. Thus He granted in full all of my pleas for help from the past through a journey back to the spiritual world that would last three and a half hours in the natural. In that spiritual place, I had no sense of time passing; it could have been weeks for all I knew. Through this process, I would find redemption, renewal, change, and be given the Armor of God described in the Book of Ephesians. I am told that with this Armor of God, I can now protect myself forever against any further attacks from the darkness and the cruelty of the shadows. It was a lot, and I'm not sure I yet understand very much of what really happened, but I know for certain that I am now free.

On that day, my understanding of the Lord's Prayer would change radically as the deliverance would alter my life forever. In my mind, the word *deliverance* used to conjure up thoughts of banjo music and a creepy movie about city boys lost in a nightmare hillbilly wilderness. Like the characters in the movie, I had been equally lost in a terrible wilderness of self-loathing and despair in my mind and in my physical existence. I had been stuck in that place for all of my life, for as far back as my memory goes. I had believed all of the lies about me and had succumbed to feelings of shame, fear, and guilt. These three feelings, in particular, had kept me chained to my past as I wrestled with an inner pain that was beyond my ability to overcome for decades. All of that was about to change radically and permanently! I had given myself a life sentence, and God was about to hand me a pardon from all of it.

The day was the twenty-sixth of May, 2011, almost five months after I started down this path. Another angel would come into my life that afternoon, one who would lead this deliverance process in a powerful way. She was truly amazing, with a quiet and gentle soul but also with the strength of a lion inside, God's lion. She presented a calm and somewhat unassuming nature to me, and to others, I would assume. Looks truly can be deceiving, because on the outside, she did not reveal the power she has on the inside to see evil and deal with it head-on in a fully spiritual way, blessed by our Creator. This quiet, gentle woman was fully able to confront the shadows directly and to stand firm in the forces they would soon throw at us in this fight. So it was that this sweet lady helped me to relax in the first moment we met. I liked and trusted her immediately.

Up to that point, I'll admit to being a bit skeptical and yet fully believing at the same time. It was an odd contradiction in myself. Yet that kind of conflict was totally normal for me so I didn't question it. I had fought this for so long and with such painful difficulty that it just seemed nearly impossible to believe I was about to really be set free from the shadows at last. Even in this, my doubt, the Spirit did not let go of me. As this day approached, I fought the skeptical leanings because I knew God had brought me to this point for my own good, so it had to have an awesome outcome somehow. The Holy Spirit was with us, and we would not be standing alone.

The little boy in me was fully on board with believing that a whole list of possibilities would come with this new freedom. He was like a kid waiting for his first trip to Disneyland. My adult side had questions of a more practical nature. Like, how does this work exactly? Where do we do this, and how do we get there? Adults reasonably question things they don't understand. Little kids just go along for the ride, anticipating fun through their innocence. I was both the adult and a little kid inside, and too often in the past, I had gone along for the ride without any regard for the bad consequences.

This time, things would be different. The conflicting expectations make sense to me now, as I had always had both sides to my personality. There was the trusting and innocent child side and the conflicted adult element. On that day, both would play a fully active role in what was to happen next, and both would be taken to the maximum level of endurance to get through it. Thus, the boy was anxious to start and take off running, while the adult was hesitant and, yes, afraid once again.

Funny thing, too; I was half expecting this new lady miracle worker was going to look at me, see evil so entrenched that I was beyond her help, and flee from me in total disgust even though God had already brought me this far. How quickly we forget what the Creator has already done. It gives me a new understanding of the disciples who saw the works of Jesus—from Jesus himself—yet they still had questions and doubts after Christ died on the cross. So it was that each side of my personality would have to be "all in" for one last trip into an unknown and frightening world where we do not naturally belong. Each would be fearful throughout the next few hours, and each would have to be brave. I would have to face the shadows once more, and I expected they would somehow be ready and waiting for me. For the first time in my life, the ladies said I would be able to *see* them in the fullness of their evil. That in itself should have been enough to stop me, but this time fear was not going to win. I had made a promise to the Spirit, and I would follow through no matter what that meant now.

Thus after visiting for a bit, this new and gentle guide in my process simply began talking to "it" or however many "its" there were inside of me. She spoke in a language I did not understand.

Just as before, when I stood at the edge of the pit where my anger had lived, I had already determined I would jump into this particular pit as well. What happened next started off calmly enough. As I write things down now, much of this day remains a blur for me, but I will describe it as best I can.

That first step was amazing. The light was about to fill my mind and erase all the places where these cowards had hidden throughout the years. With their shield of darkness gone, they would get very angry with me, the little boy, and the ladies, too. As noted, I didn't know that was coming, but it didn't matter anyway. If humans can see into some part of the spiritual world, I was about to do so, though I would be surrounded this time by the full light of God and not the darkness I had experienced before. That light would show me the things I needed to see and give me the strength I needed.

Nonetheless, what followed would be painful and difficult. I was to see things from two vantage points. One on the outside of myself and one on the inside, at the same time, with both sides fighting hard and fighting back. This time, the little boy would stay close and hide behind the grown-up man as the following events progressed, and he was soon to be very terrified. And so it was the process began.

Chapter THIRTEEN

"Because he loves me," says the Lord, "I will rescue him. I will protect him, for he acknowledges my name. He will call on me and I will answer him. I will be with him in trouble. I will deliver him and honor him. With long life I shall honor him, and show him my salvation."

Psalm 91:14–16

THE BATTLE BEGINS

Without fully realizing it, I'd jumped into the pit once more. The new angel's words flooded my mind, and with them came a pure and brilliant light that exposed everything. It shown brightly on all the shadows in all of their vile forms, and they could hide no more. Even if I could describe their horrific nature now, I would not do so. That would give them honor they do not deserve. I thank God anyway that those images are gone from my mind. I learned through this with certainty that they were all real, as I had always suspected them to be even though they had tried hard to make me doubt their existence. It was an attempt to confuse me and drive me back toward despair and sadness. It didn't work this time.

Nope, I knew they were real, and now it was confirmed with my being able to see them. These demonic spirits that had stayed hidden from me for years were now forced to fully identify themselves by the command of a more powerful servant of God. Three would eventually say their names, and the others had an "identity" more tied to their function. I only remember one of the names in writing this, but to speak that name again only gives the thing another chance to come back or feel good about its cruelty. My counselor tells me they cannot read my mind and only God can do that. So if I think its name, this shadow does not know, but if I speak it, well, that is a different story and not one I want to revisit ever again.

I recall she started speaking next directly to the shadows, praying in a language I didn't understand, as I mentioned, then switching back to English. She took on the strongest of them first, demanding that it tell her *its* name. To me, she gently said I was to repeat whatever I'd heard in my head, no matter how nonsensical it seemed, and just let it come out. I heard a name, all right, more than once, too, as it finally spat out of my mouth in a cowardly little hiss. Its name was barely audible to me, but clearly, she heard it. Still the coward I thought, but now this entity was forced to obey a servant of God and identify itself. On hearing its name, she calmly said, *"Oh, it's you again."*

Really? She had encountered this thing somewhere before? Where and how often, I have no idea, but she knew it, and had faced it down previously. It would lose the fight again on that day, too, but not without putting up a very strong defense first. With each of her commands, it pulled at me on the inside, clinging to my soul with what felt like multiple tentacles clutching tightly, using a powerful grip. Strong, yes, but not stronger then God. Ultimately, it would lose that hold on me. This would take time as whatever this thing was, it clearly was strong. Once this started, the boy became more afraid than he had ever been before, even more fearful then on that previous day when I had decided to leap into my anger and confront it. His eagerness to start a few moments earlier was fully gone now, and who can blame him after what just happened and what we were seeing now. He begged the adult me, and the angels too, to make it stop.

"They'll come back; they'll hurt us again. Make her stop!" he cried.

I could not do so even if had I tried or wanted to. She continued her firm commands, and along with them, his terror echoed in my mind at the same time. It was my own fear from the past speaking as this boy's pleas called from behind the grown-up me, standing in this spiritual place with no floors, walls, or ceiling. It was just me, this bright white space, and them. Christ was there, though I do not recall seeing Him, yet He had to be the source of this brilliant light. I think I repeated the boy's pleas out loud, and I'm sure the ladies understood their source at once.

In response, this new angel replied with a firm, "NO!" She spoke in the way a parent would speak to a child who wants nothing but cake for dinner. It was nonetheless said with total love, and I knew that, he knew that. It was the kind of no that a child cannot understand but will accept, and we did. As she continued her work with commands, she also told me that later, they would not come back, and now, they could not hurt me anymore unless I willingly let them do so. It was a reassurance that this horrid process would be worth the effort. I understood and was satisfied with that answer fully, knowing it was the truth no matter what was coming next. The adult me needed this reinforcement as much as the little kid me needed it, because I was now equally terrified as the fight continued.

With that issue addressed, she fully returned to the shadow and focused her commands at full strength toward it. The whole thing was incredible, really. Could this possibly have been the same woman who seemed so gentle the moment before? Now she had taken off the quiet outer robe and presented a fully armored representative of Christ. If I had the presence of mind to think about it, I'd have said, "You go, girl! Kick some butt! Slaughter them!" Of course "it" tried to ignore her, and she pressed harder on the shadows as they fought back against her with equal tenacity.

"You have no power here. In the name of Jesus, I order you to identify yourself."

After the thing submitted and said its name, she commanded it to leave, yet it still resisted with all of its strength, draining mine in the same moment. Confronted by her strength from Christ, it could not refuse the command. When we operate in the Spirit, one more powerful than the unholy master of darkness is giving the orders, and that was true on this day. Having been forced to speak its name, this first and strongest of the shadows spat vile words into my mind in response to *her*. Things I would never say to a woman or anyone, really, it was trying to force me to say to her, and I resisted. It said to hit her, along with other things I will not describe. Not that she would have been phased in the least had I done any of that. She knew it was them and not me fighting back.

In these moments, I had enough fight and control still left in me to refuse to repeat that garbage. Maybe some of my lingering anger helped me here because from my vantage point, I flat out refused to let my mouth repeat "its" words. That language wasn't coming out of my mouth anymore if I could stop it, and I did.

Again, I pictured Gandalf in the mines in *The Lord of the Rings*, and forced a reply back to it, saying, *"You shall not pass,"* referring to the words it tried to force into my mouth. I was fighting as hard on the inside as the angels were fighting on the outside with their prayers and commands. They tell me that I growled at them, and that as this battle raged on, my face changed radically then changed back to normal, like some sign that I was fighting inside. And I was. I could feel the changes in me physically but could not stop that part totally. I'm equally sure I had angry eyes again, piercing with a malevolence expressed by *it* and not by me. I could not stop that, but I could stop the words. This would only get worse.

On and on the ladies prayed and commanded the thing at the same time, pulling out its tentacles that held fast with any number of claws in different parts of my mind and soul. It had no more darkness in which to hide and was fully exposed. I tried not to look at it while its grasp weakened and its desperation increased, trying in vain to refuse the orders. Surely this was not the first time if had been removed from someone, and it must have lost the battle each and every time. How could it, this thing, think that it could win now? Regardless, the thing was stubborn, and worse, it was getting very angry. More foul language, more growls, and more hate flew around in my mind like so many arrows coming from all directions. All of it directed at the two women, me, and the little boy hiding behind me. My smaller self, not able to understand at all, was terrified. I cannot recall seeing Jesus in these tense moments, but He was there. I am certain of that, thank God.

As the first shadow finally lost its grip and was pulled from me, it came out in a heavy exhale of evil as it left my physical body like some sort of venomous exhaust. I have no idea how many of the pulled breaths it took; I was too distracted, and who could think to keep any sort of count in that place. My counselor had told me the way these things are forced to leave is different for everyone. Some people will scream, some will sigh, belch, giggle, or whatever. For me, it was that terrible breath being pulled from my lungs as she extracted the last of their energy out of me. Her commands, the ones I could hear or understand, sounded something like "Come on, leave; you cannot refuse." Time suspended, but finally the first of the shadows was at last gone and out of me forever. I don't know where it went, but it would no longer find refuge inside of me. One down, the most powerful of them all, but this was only the beginning. There would be eleven more to deal with, and they would not give up easily either.

Before that moment, I absolutely had no memory of when that thing was not a part of me. Now, after so many years, it was gone, finally gone. I cannot express any words to describe how good that feels. In that moment, I drew even closer to God. I don't deserve it, but His love is not given based on what we deserve. He just gives it without condition, as He did with me in that moment. The day was not over and I already felt drained, very tired, and knew that though this was only the beginning but it was an amazing confirmation of God's ultimate power.

At some point, she addressed the white spider from my dreams. I thought it had gone long ago, as I'd not seen it for years. Oh no, it was still there. She prayed and addressed it directly. It was to be the one thing that I actually saw leaving me. From out of my center, it clearly emerged, transparent, but fully in the form I had seen in so many nightmares. No longer able to hide, out it came, scurried across the floor, and ran away right through the closed door, gone for good. I remember sitting up on one elbow and watching its escape. I tried to explain what I'd seen, but neither of the two ladies saw the ghostly spider leave me and walk out of the room. They told that was for my benefit alone, so I would know this was real, as if I didn't have evidence enough already. After it was gone, I collapsed again, falling back into the world where the rest of the shadows remained, defiant.

At one point, she prayed something about me being released from the chains of false beliefs throughout the years. Her words said something about being free from the lies I'd learned at four to ten years old, then to twenty years old, and so on. I remember begging her to keep going. From my place, wherever it was, I knew this was working. I'm not sure how I communicated that but do recall saying something, though I was not sure it was loud enough for the ladies to hear me. They did, praise God, and we moved on. It was another step completed, leaving me more exhausted and drained, but also renewed at the same time, somehow, as this process continued.

We came to a point where my exhaustion started to take its toll. I have no idea how long we had been doing this, but all I wanted to do was sleep, just simply sleep. I had no more energy inside, at least none that I could find, and I remember mumbling something about going to sleep. I even tried to turn onto my side and nap, but the ladies would have none of that. They steadfastly refused to let me doze off. I pretty much recall being told I was not going to sleep, not now. They would not permit it, in spite of my pleas. I, or it, fought them but they were persistent, so I managed to stay awake. I felt like the little boy was in front now, and protesting. In this moment, both the ladies sounded like moms, and they were pretty clear.

"No, you are not going to sleep. We've got work to do," they said, almost in unison.

"OK, I'll stay awake!" was my answer and I must have sounded like an annoyed teenager. I was really tired yet stayed with them. I had to in order for this to be done.

Immediately after that, I started to get extremely cold all over, inside and out. I've been in survival training where the overnight temps went down to -70 with the wind chill. On this warm May afternoon, I felt colder than even that, with an intensity that went right through to my core. It was as if the room temperature had dropped 120 degrees in an instant. The ladies did not feel it, but I did and began to shiver violently. In previous sessions, my counselor had identified a death wish in me, and that is what I was confronting now. This thing, I didn't see, though I expected it to be visible and like some specter in the cartoons of the skeleton in robes carrying a scythe. I had beaten the suicide thoughts years before, but the death wish was still there, I guess, in some form. I said something about being cold. As the ladies worked, the chill got worse. My counselor gave me a blanket.

They prayed as I shivered, and I don't remember much more except that it went away almost as quickly as it had started. It left me too. Later my counselor told me the coldness tried to latch onto her, as an icy cloak descending on her from above for a brief moment. She commanded it to leave and it did, knowing it had no power to possess her either. Still, it tried, and it lost once again. How stupid can these things be? Pretty stupid apparently, as they keep failing until they find a victim who cannot fight them.

They had found me and been there for years, but God had different plans. Sadly, I am sure they will find another child to haunt into adulthood as they did with me. I am very saddened by that, and I don't understand it. Even so, I do know that God remains in charge, and in the end, they are going to lose forever no matter where they try to hide. On this day, they lost control over me for sure and forever.

The presence of death lingered in that room even after the dark spirit left me. Before it left, death whispered terrible things to me. It said that I could go, but, *"The boy is mine; the boy is dead."*

Inside, this terrified me, and I could not speak these words as they came to me when I reported to the ladies. My small and innocent self was now totally afraid that the adult side would leave him in that awful place with that awful thing. Again, he pleaded with me to take us both away. He wanted to run and hide anywhere, but there was no place to hide. The brilliant light had eliminated every dark place. The light was our shield anyway, and the darkness had only provided a hiding spot for the shadows in my past. I certainly was not going to leave him, me, behind to continue living in that nightmare. So he stayed close, and we all fought on.

The ladies' prayers continued, and I wondered how much more of this we could endure. It was almost like all the years of pain and sadness were flooding back in one giant ball of hurt resting on me. Eventually, I was more exhausted, but no longer afraid. The death wish, or spirit, or whatever it was had finally left us and could not return. Others remained, and the difficult process moved forward into the afternoon as time stood frozen to me.

– Twelve Shadows, Twelve Faces of Evil –

I'll admit this has got to sound strange to a lot of people, so I don't offer just my own word to the validity of these events. I know what happened, and I support my story of this battle with scripture. Ephesians 6:12 says this. *For our struggle is not against flesh and blood, but against the rulers, against the authorities, against the powers of this dark world, and against the spiritual forces of evil in the heavenly realms.*

On that day, I counted twelve of these things, these shadows that the angels pulled out of me. No, I was not possessed by them but I was connected to them somehow. The first one had a name. Then came the death spirit, the white spider and the rest in turn. All were connected to my own history. To this day, I'm not sure how they all worked or how they entered and lived in me, except that abuse allowed some sort of access to them. Their control would ultimately end on that spring afternoon, but we were not quite done yet.

One of the last of the spirits to be addressed by the ladies was that of a small boy, but not me. He was someone I remember playing with when I was little, sometime during the years the men were molesting me. He lived in an old, Victorian-era house, and I remember he showed me a hidden panel in the kitchen of the home. It was a small hiding spot for valuables built invisibly into the wooden trim at countertop level. Later, when I was in elementary school, we took a field trip to that house. It was a museum then, and the guide told us there was a hidden panel in the kitchen, adding "But I bet you boys and girls can't find it." I went right to it and showed her. She asked how I knew it was there, and I told her I'd learned of it from the little boy who used to live there, while we were playing.

She then answered, *"Sweetheart, no one has lived in this house for eighty years."*

I still have images of the little boy I played with. His clothes were different, but not that much different than mine, as I recall. Today, I wonder if he was actually a caretaker's son or something like that, or if he was something else from the other side. I never felt any fear around him, not once. Even so, the ladies prayed for him, and me, and I think he was maybe the last of the spirits to be released from me. My hope is that he was released from whatever tie he had to me to move on into the light if he was indeed a child's spirit, that his spirit found its way to heaven and into God's loving arms.

– Freedom Found –

It was finally over. I was back to being fully in myself once more along with being dehydrated and utterly worn out. I've never felt that tired and drained of all my strength. As it ended, I fell onto my back in the small room at the church, looked at the ladies, and through more tears just quietly said:

"I'm free."

I was and I knew it. Knew it with absolute certainty. I would no longer be subjected to the great sadness that had been played out in my life and mind for so many years. From that point forward, nothing could ever attack me again from the inside. I would now have strength to deal with spiritual things that would come at me from the outside, but their hold inside me was gone. Now I could start to heal.

My counselor had taught me about putting on the Armor of God as described in the Book of Ephesians. Feeling like I had cleaned out a deep wound and survived the process, I was ready in that moment to put on the armor. I was finally, fully, and forever…free.

God had kept his promise given when I started this, and for the first time in my life, I felt a sense of real peace deep down inside. It was one like I have never known before. In that moment, I also looked for the boy, the younger me. In my mind, I found him at last sleeping quietly and securely in a warm light in the palm of Christ's hand. I can see him there today, safe, loved, and never to hurt again like he had so much before in the natural. It makes me smile. He is the memory of a small me who lived afraid of the world. Today, his fear and sadness are gone and replaced with a new image. The adult me can move forward with a confidence I have never known before. No shadows will ever torment him (or me) again from their hiding places in my mind. They will try from the outside, but it's no use. Their grip on my spirit is broken.

The date was Thursday, May 26, 2011. My life's course had altered forever on that warm afternoon in the comforting presence of the two angels who had done so much for me on God's behalf. When I went to sleep later that night, the shadows were gone from my dreams. I slept in true peace for the first time in decades, knowing that they could no longer walk in my dreams. Thank you, Jesus.

Chapter FOURTEEN

The human race has only one really effective weapon and that is laughter. The moment it arises, all your irritations and resentments slip away and the sunny spirit takes their place.

Mark Twain

HEAR THE FROGS SINGING!

I can laugh again for real now, and I can feel that joy inside that comes from it, too. The sunny spirit at the source for me is the Holy Spirit. I believe that laughter is a gift from God and that it acts as a release valve for joy. For me, the "spirit" that Mr. Twain refers to has to be the Holy Spirit. It just has to be. That night, I slept in total peace for the first time in years, my whole life in fact. No more would the shadows, white spiders, ginger dogs with flaming eyes, and evil shapes invade my sleep.

Bad dreams may come again, but it won't be like before as I am no longer helplessly subject to their manipulations. So if they try, I am ready for them. I was at peace, totally, and that is the only way I can describe how I felt the day following my deliverance process. As bad as it was living with the shadows, this new sense of me is a total 180-degree difference and the joy is far more intense than the pain-filled sadness. Of course I still have other concerns in life. Unemployment, stress over everyday things that living throws at us, etc., but none of that matters now. Those things cannot defeat me or define me. I am restored and transformed and celebrating with strength I did not know could exist in me.

I woke the next morning with the same feeling of total joy and the sense of a new purpose in my heart! God's message to me was that I now have new eyes, but what that means, I still don't know. I've asked Him, and the Spirit says I'll know more when it's time and when I'm ready. OK, I'll accept that, as He's never failed to deliver thus far. That morning, I went to mow the grass at the church and had to stop several times while circling the lawn. My new happiness kept overwhelming me and I'd start crying, but this time, tears of joy as an expression of my thanks to God. A mowing job that normally took an hour and a half took almost three hours this time. I didn't care.

I just kept saying it out loud to myself...I'M FREE. With that praise, I'd dance a jig around the lawnmower and anyone who saw me must have thought the church hired a total loon to mow their grass, but I didn't care about that either and still don't. No words that I can think of are remotely adequate to say what I was feeling. I had a new, strong, and purposeful relationship with God. The great sadness was gone along with the shadows, and I could move forward now. I knew it, too.

After finishing up the lawn, I went home and decided the dog and I needed a walk. That was also to be an amazing experience. We don't normally think of walking the dog as amazing, but this time, it was. Near our home is a small wetland running through the open space. The spring rains and snow runoff had made the cattails, reeds and rushes green up beautifully. Here it was in the middle of the day, and I had to stop in my tracks when the dog and I got to the wetlands as I could not believe what I was hearing. Had God given me new ears, too? I could hear the frogs singing, which is not their normal habit in the middle of the afternoon. What a beautiful sound.

All of my senses were heightened on that afternoon, and even the sunlight seemed more vibrant. Colors around me were stunning, along with the sights and sounds of what was, on the surface, just an ordinary day to everyone else. There was nothing ordinary about it to me at all, not in that moment. Emotions welled up in me, and I had to say it again…I'M FREE! This time, I did so without my little dance. I was in awe. What an incredible blessing to see something so beautiful in a world that had been merely ordinary, or even painful, before. It was like seeing the world for the first time, which was very true because my image of it had been transformed totally.

On arriving back home, my counselor called to check in on me. I'd sent her an e-mail earlier, between jigs, but she had not checked her inbox yet that day. I described for her what had been happening and how tired I still was. My typical high level of energy had been put to good use mowing the church lawn and walking the dog. Now sitting on our porch, I felt drained again but still so very joyful.

We discussed the day before and I told her what the voice had told me. I told her that it had said, *"You can go but the boy is mine, and he is dead."* They were still liars in the midst of all that was going on, but they lost in the end. I told her about the other things the shadows had tried to get me to say to them, foul-mouthed garbage, and how one had told me to hit them both.

She said her friend had commented that the man seemed to want to fight but the little boy was more difficult. I told her that he is sleeping now and described how I see him in my mind, there in the palm of Christ's hand. For me, that image of myself at six years old is safe, and he will never be hunted or hurt again.

Frogs and colors I had not seen or heard before. What an amazing day, truly amazing.

Chapter FIFTEEN

Do not weep! See, the Lion of the tribe of Judah,
the Root of David, has triumphed!

Revelation 5:5

Eighteen Months Later

WHAT NOW, LORD?

Those days immediately following my deliverance were joy-filled, with the sights and sounds and warmth of God's love. It is impossible to describe this transformation and really do it any kind of justice. Many times, I had heard people say they were completely changed by an encounter with Jesus. Scripture describes it that way too. Look at what happened to Paul on that road to Damascus. Yet until this time, it had not happened in me in any measurable way that I could recognize. Well, that is exactly what Christ is able to do in us, redeem, transform, and make us new. Some days, I cannot believe the new me I see in the mirror, but I will take him.

The above verse means so much to me. The Lion of Judah is my companion now. Like the lion character Aslan in *The Chronicles of Narnia* stories, He gently leads and guides me. I still need that, perhaps now more than ever before. I am not the person I was inside, or outside, for that matter. I have lost nearly forty-five pounds and feel great about my new self physically. God kept His word, and has taken what was meant for my harm and turned it to something good, as scripture promises He will do. I'll work hard to repay the price paid by Christ on the cross. I cannot really repay it, of course, but I can try, and even more important I really want to try. I know there is more to come, more things I have to face with the Spirit and my counselor. More tears, too, as I still cry, but this will not last forever, again as scripture promises.

The intensity of colors and sounds that I had experienced after my deliverance were to fade. Not to something bad, just back to something normal. It was not meant to be a permanent experience. Perhaps God had given me a glimpse into heaven. With certainty, I know I can look forward to the day when I'll hear the frogs again along with seeing more colors, hearing more sounds, and finding more freedom. Someday, I shall see it all again, and all the more intensely too. For now, I have a "new normal" and a new definition of myself and life. Eventually, as things settled down, I knew that it was time to start the healing process. I had no idea what that would require either, yet this new road was a safe one though probably no less bumpy. Looking back on where I was before, this will only keep getting better. I'll take it.

It reminds me of the 1990s, when massive wildfires devastated the landscape in Yellowstone National Park, leaving behind a blackened, barren piece of ground that looked dead on the surface. Yet the fire had cleaned up years of lifeless branches, scrub brush, weeds and waste that kept the land from producing to its full potential. That image is how I see myself now, following my deliverance.

The Spirit's fire cleansed me inside and out. What had been a wasteland of sadness in my soul was now cleared away, and my spirit man had changed. This me is all new thanks to the Holy Spirit. He gets the credit. It's true I made the choice to follow Him, but that transformation was *His* touch, and no one can rob me of that now. Nor can they create an illusion they have taken it, just like the illusion of my innocence being permanently destroyed because of the predators. Christ's work on the cross restored that. I have learned, too, that becoming free and healing are two entirely different things. My freedom was instant on that May afternoon in 2011, but my healing would take time, and it would go hand in hand with my growing relationship with Jesus in sanctification.

All of the weeds and dead branches of the past were gone. He has truly begun a new work in me. Even before I knew it, God had begun to remake me into who he intended me to be in the first place. Bit by bit, God is chipping away at this marble block that is the unrefined me. I don't know how soon or when, but He will reveal His version of me. I think it is also OK that this will take time. As my pastor told me, my freedom in Christ is instant but my growth in him will be a lifelong process. I'm not really sure what that means, but I guess I'll find out.

The landscape in Yellowstone has recovered now. It is vibrant with new trees, shrubs and wildlife inhabiting the places cleaned out by the fire years before. In the same way, I feel new and vibrant again, too. Just like it has taken some time for the land to recover and heal, the same will be true with me. I am no longer working on being set free, I am working on being made new.

– A New Mission –

I am called now to testify. The words I heard at the start of this come back to me, echoing my counselor's prediction that I would be speaking publicly, and my insistence that wasn't going to happen. That thinking has changed in me, like everything else. The idea both excites and frightens me at the same time. How do I speak about my past struggles in public, things that had been kept buried for most of my life? Yet the Holy Spirit has called me to do it as a way to help others. I don't know the words to use even, so I told the Spirit I would open my mouth if He would put the words in me. His answer to my prayer was a simple, "OK." So I would be in this race set out before me, no matter where it would lead.

I have now spoken about the abuse and my path to freedom at four churches and two Christian conferences. I also recorded a video testimony at the request of my church for their Easter 2015 services. On that day some 5,000 people heard me speak. My counselor sat beside me during the service as I watched and listened to my own words on the large monitors in our sanctuary. It made me tear up, not out of shame or regret, but thanks to the Spirit who had led me to this point.

I was to realize something important about this video recording. In truth, I really do not like having my picture taken, because people had taken my pictures in a bad way when I was little. It was one more episode I would have to work through in counseling. When the church called and said the head pastor had asked if I would do a video testimony, it never occurred to me to say no.

If my church was asking, I would do it. It was a very easy decision in the moment that I do not regret. Several months prior to this request, the Spirit had told me it was time to take back my image, because my image never belonged to them in the first place. It always belonged to God. I knew what this meant, but I had no idea how it would come about. Scripture says where we may not see a way, God has already made a way, and He had done so in this, too. I was willing, even if I had no clue how it would happen.

On the day we recorded that video, I sat there with several cameras pointed at me, answering questions and was at total peace inside doing so. The session lasted roughly fifteen minutes, as I talked to the pastor there who ran the media department. He is yet another incredible man of God in that church, along with so many other men and women. Walking out afterward, I stopped in my tracks, realizing in that moment that I...me...the one who does not like my picture taken, had sat there in peace. Nothing about doing that had triggered me, nor did the idea that it would be shown to so many people on Easter Sunday of 2015.

The thought of it being shown on the big screen was overwhelming and comforting at the same time. About a month later, I realized God had walked me through something without my even having realized it. How can we even begin to understand that? It is His amazing love at work yet again, and all I can say is, "Wow; thank you, Jesus."

It was not my first testimony, but was my first put on video and made permanent. The first time I spoke was less than a year after my deliverance process, when my counselor and her friend called me about speaking. Her friend's Pentecostal church was hosting a conference on the demonic and deliverance, and they wanted to know if I would be willing to share some of my story. I immediately said yes, but after hanging up the phone, it hit me. The prospect of talking in front of a group about all of that scared me. So I fired off an e-mail to them saying I really could not do this as I was still fearful, had no idea what to say, etc., etc. They accepted my withdrawal graciously, of course, with understanding and said that it was OK if I was not ready. So much for that plan, as the Spirit came around to give me a good talking to about my decision. The whole conversation struck me as sort of a parental lecture and was kind of new to me. It went something like this:

"So, these ladies have helped you get free, and now that they need your help, you're going to just turn your back on them? Of course, it's your choice whether to help them or not."

"I can't do this, not yet," was my reply. And that was the essence of this short conversation.

His message was loud and clear but not spoken in anger. I thought it wasn't fair, with my excuses lined up. I've discovered we make excuses with God, even after all He's done for us. I kept thinking about it as the voice of the Holy Spirit is never wrong, and as I have learned, it should not be ignored either. Even so, how could He possibly want me to do this? I had no idea what I could say or even where and how to start. So I got clever in my mind and decided I would craft a reply to see what He thought about that. I told Him I was afraid, that I did not have the right words, etc., and then I said:

"OK, I'll do this, stand up and open my mouth, if You put the words in it."

My thinking was that the Spirit's response would be something like, *"Well, if you don't know the words, I won't give them to you. You'll have to think them up when you're ready,"* and that would get me out of having to speak. Of course, it did not dawn on me that God invented words, knew them all in any language you could pick. He is more than capable of giving me the right ones to say, if I would be willing to try. God already knew what I would say in response to my counselor and her friend. Once again, His love and understanding would be evident even if I didn't see it in the moment. Thus again after presenting my argument and proposed deal, I immediately saw one word in my mind in huge letters. That word is one I've gotten before:

"Agreed."

Now I had to do it, as I made the offer and God had accepted my proposal. He could have called down thunder and lightning to terrify me into submission, or He could have made me blind until I repented, but He didn't do any of that. God just agreed, quietly and in love. That's all there is to that. Unlike the last time I had this kind of talk with the Spirit, during my search for anger, nothing in me felt like I'd been maneuvered into this position or wondered if I'd been tricked. This time, with a new fullness, I understood that if God said He would give me the words, then He would do just that. Having never experienced anything like this before, I still found myself nervous and excited about speaking in public for the first time and wondered how God would do this. Ultimately, it was to be an amazing experience in ways I did not even expect, as God was to use me on that day for more than just speaking.

– God Only Knows –

On the day of the conference, my counselor spoke first. She talked about her process and the people with whom she has worked, leading up to my introduction. It was then my turn. I got up and put on a headset, as I like to have both hands free while speaking, then turned to face a room of maybe forty people, all watching me with great expectation. They were not the only ones. A year before that day, I could not even say the word *molested* to my counselor. I felt that I had no right to even think it back then, and believed it was something I deserved. Back then, I still clung to the lies of the enemy on that and on so many other issues, too. A year before that conference, I lived in fear of words, yet standing there, it was a different feeling. I took a breath, knowing the Spirit had promised to give me words. I was about to say *molested* out loud to a group of total strangers, and many other words as well, in telling how I had come to be there on that warm spring day.

With my hands free and natural hyper energy kicking in, I first explained that I would have to pace around while telling my story since standing still is something I'm not very good at. As kind faces looked on, not really knowing what to expect, I still had no clue either as to what I would say. I just opened my mouth and started to speak. My story about the events came out first along with how I had fought the shadows for years. It was followed by how none of my own efforts to fix it had worked. I then talked about getting into counseling with God's help and how difficult that process was. After that, I spoke about the deliverance process and what I had felt (and seen) during that day, including one of the demons actually coming out of me. I told them about feeling very tired, cold, angry, and afraid throughout the process.

My testimony continued, and it turned to my first journey into the spiritual world, about how dark it was that time and how it was where I had to confront anger, which was the source of that darkness. I told them that in the end, my anger would be replaced with the light of God as I approached the cross for the first time, about forgiveness. As

I spoke about seeing the shadows unmasked during my last journey to the spiritual realm, this group already knew that such shadows couldn't hide in that light, yet they listened to me with compassion.

Parts of this presentation brought me to tears as recalling it still hurt enough to do so, and at one point, I had to put my head down on the podium for a few seconds to recharge. Those seconds felt like an eternity. All of this came out as people looked on in supportive silence. I finally got to a stopping point, but did not know how. Thankfully, the pastor running the program recognized it, stood up, and hugged me. It was over, my first testimony. I returned to my seat, stunned and exhausted inside, but knowing fully that both God and I had kept the respective parts of our bargain. Of course, God will always keep his promises to us. This was all the proof I needed that He had been and would be with me from then on.

I thought it was done for that day and was happy about the presentation. We had risen to the challenge expected of me. The next person to speak was my counselor's friend, who told of her own abuse. Her story is vastly different from mine, but I have learned that while victims of abuse have unique experiences, we have shared hurts. I could relate to her pain as she spoke. Her sister was there as well, and she had also been abused.

While she was speaking, some "thing" had come to the conference, uninvited. It was demonic, and it immediately went into her sister, who fled the room instantly. My counselor's friend had to stop speaking right then and go to help. In turn, my counselor quickly got up to go with her and invited me to come along. I just said there was nothing I could do, so I stayed behind. Off they went, and again, the Holy Spirit came to me, this time to ask or gently push me to help the ladies.

"I don't know what to do," I told the Spirit, no longer paying attention to what was going on in the room. He then showed me a scene from a television miniseries I'd seen as a little kid, called *Jesus of Nazareth*. I remembered it well. Jesus was commanding a demon to leave a man in the temple, I think. In that scene, Christ simply said, *"Leave him!"*

"That is all you need to do," the Spirit gently told me; just those words and nothing more. Sitting there, physically and emotionally worn out, I was not intentionally trying to be stubborn but was just still very unsure of myself, even though I had no doubt about God's ability to take care of the demon active in the next room. After discussing this with the Spirit for who knows how long, suddenly, I found myself getting up and heading toward the room. I was not doing this under my own power, either, but was being moved physically by the Spirit since I would not go willingly. I got to the room and opened the door. Immediately, one of the women looked at me and said, *"Good, he's here."*

What? Clearly she had known I would be coming even if I hadn't. Then she looked at me and commanded, *"Just do it!"*

I have learned not to argue with church ladies of any denomination, so I looked at the two women struggling with whatever it was, laid my hands on them both, and said the words I'd been given.

"LEAVE HER!"

With that, I felt a tremendous energy rush through my arms, out of my hands, and into them. Whatever it was, it was instantly gone. In a flash, I was back in control of myself once more. The two ladies and I snapped out of it at the same time as they were freed from the struggle they had been enduring seconds before. We looked at each other in stunned, silent amazement.

In that moment, I had done what the Holy Spirit told me to do, even if He did have to drag me in there to do it. I love that about the Spirit. I also knew that *I* had not really done anything at all except be the messenger. My counseling had taught me that the authority to command such things comes from God alone and not me. It was that very point that got me to worrying later, too. I called my counselor and asked her about this concern. After all, I had been taught that we are to command things to leave in the name of Jesus, using words like, *"In Jesus's name, I bind you up and command you to go back to the void from which you came."* I had not said that, but only *"Leave her."*

My counselor asked me what I had been told to say. That was it, came my reply, just those two words. She pointed out I had done what I was told, and that all the others in that room were issuing commands in Christ's name as well so that was covered. I was satisfied with the answer. Whatever that thing was, it knew that the Holy Spirit was there and He had commanded it to go, not me. The demon was powerless to refuse. I prayed on it, too, and the Spirit told me later I am correct to remember to do things in His name in the future, but I had not made a mistake on that day, as I had obeyed His direction. It would be yet another totally new experience to me to add to a growing list.

At the end of the conference, several people came up to me to say they were moved by my story, words and tears. They were God's words, really. These kind people told me they were also inspired to reach out and get help for struggles in their own lives after hearing me speak. Through their kindness, I started to learn on that day how God would use me to help others. Several more times since then, the Holy Spirit has reminded me that I am a survivor for a reason, and that God really can take something evil and turn it into something good. He's God; of course He can.

The next time I spoke was more recently, to members of the same church that had held the conference. I needed to go as the pastor had invited me, and they had prayed for me on my day of deliverance. I owed them that thanks and considerably more, too, and I needed to say it publicly. That night, I spoke briefly to express my gratitude for their support and a little about what God had been doing in my life since that day. I closed with a reference to a scripture verse I had learned recently. It is Psalm 91:14–16:

"Because he loves me," says the Lord, "I will rescue him; I will protect him, for he acknowledges my name. He will call on me and I will answer him; I will be with him in trouble, I will deliver him and honor him. With long life I will satisfy him and show him my salvation."

It was yet another good night, and a good learning experience. I am seeing now that every time I speak, it is getting easier to tell my story. It also gives me back a part of myself, helps others who are listening, and mostly draws us all closer to God.

– A Safe Challenge –

As excited as I am to speak, several people have warned me to be careful about sharing my story. That advice confused me, so I asked why. They tell me that some people will make assumptions about me, knowing I grew up in abuse. More simply put, some people believe that most (if not all) boys who are abused will grow up to become predators themselves. I was, and I still am, stunned at that bit of news. I could never hurt a child as I was hurt, and never hit anyone so violently except maybe in self-defense. Nor do I verbally abuse people with the words and labels that were flung at me. At times, I still get defensive and don't communicate love well, as a reflection of Christ, but I am learning to defeat this problem, too. None of that abuse I experienced is inside of me to hurt others, yet I'm told some will just assume it is there. Why?

It leaves me to wonder how could people think that way. It is like yet another label being slammed on me by people who have not experienced what happened to me and who don't get how it hurts when they say that sort of thing. Maybe they don't want to understand it, as the subject is painful to talk about. Try having lived with it. It is painful and victims of abuse do not deserve more labels. We have had more than enough of those already.

One person candidly told me, *"Well, statistically, it's true when it comes to broken boys growing up to be predators."* The argument goes like this: Most of the offenders in prisons admit to having been abused. So there you go, all victims grow up to be abusers. Baloney! All that tells me is that many of them were victims, and some did in fact grow up to continue the sad cycle. However, there is no evidence I've seen to show that *all* abuse victims grow into predators. I read recently that the average predator in prison has some 225 victims before they get caught; so one person can cause a lot of pain. I have talked to so many other survivors, I know these ideas are flat out wrong and I will fight that myth as well. Knowing what I do about God now, I will even say without hesitation that He can change them, too. OK, so I will have to be careful in sharing my story, but I will share it and not live in fear of what people think. No weapon formed against me will stand as long as my words reflect what God has done for me.

At the same time, it's totally understandable that parents can worry, so I will not volunteer to work with the children's ministry at church. I can and will help in other ways where God directs me, and will not back down from speaking as I have seen clearly how it helps others. I am certain there are many people out there still trapped by the lies I used to believe thanks to the enemy being hard at work. This fight is taken to the enemy now, with me wearing the Armor of God described in Ephesians. I can win the battles in His name as long as I remain totally subject to His authority. Another person said that sounds like I'm boasting. I boast of nothing but the Cross of Christ. I will be a soldier in His army, in whatever capacity that He directs. It is that simple. No matter how uncomfortable people get from hearing about how evil is active in this world, my job is to keep testifying and in that, glorifying what Jesus has done for me. If people have an issue with my testimony, it is their problem not mine.

As for labels, I believe that too many people go through life wearing labels others have placed on them, not just through abuse but sometime simply because of negative things spoken over them by coworkers, parents, teachers and others. One of the most powerful things I learned in counseling is that abusers are good at putting labels on their victims to get control over them. For the perpetrator, it is all about control when they do it. All of us can label others, as I know I have done so, too, without the intent of abuse, but the result is the same. In writing this, I stopped to ask God's forgiveness for my sins there and ask that He remove the negative results of my words from those whom I misjudged. Then I asked Him to help me remember to guard my words in the future.

Children are especially vulnerable to the label tactic, and it is one of the best tricks of the enemy. I had many labels attached to me and had simply accepted them until God showed me His view in a different light. Predators will of course tell you "this" is what you are good at and it is what you are good for. Your identity becomes that and nothing else. In other places, people told me that I was lazy or not smart enough to go to college and that I did not have any talent for the art that I loved creating. Yet even when I was still in the trap, God gave me the ability to push forward and not totally believe what others said over me. I did not know at the time that He was helping me there, too, but He was.

When God led me to my counselors and I learned about the traps and the ungodly beliefs such as labels from the enemy, I was able to tear them off in time. Some days, it is still a fight for me not to buy into the labels once again, and I have to remind myself that those things never applied to me. So now I wear the labels God has given me and always intended for me, such as child of the one true King or that "I am a masterpiece. I am fearfully and wonderfully made." I am not bad, ordinary or average, because I am a unique creation in Him. I am redeemed, forgiven, renewed and transformed through Christ. I am His, and He loves me for who I am. Perfect in the natural? No, but I am loved and it's for real.

By the way, I will get back to painting with watercolors, just for the pure joy of doing it. It will be just as I have done with my writing, which is another passion. While I may be down in the moment with being unemployed, I am not done. God has a plan and I will find a new place with an employer who will value my sense of character and integrity. When the bad labels come back into my mind, I will take those thoughts captive and remind myself that it does not matter what others say or have said about me, it only matters what God says, and it is not over for anyone until He says so.

That is why I will continue to testify now when asked. I made a promise to the Holy Spirit to speak when His direction comes for me there. I was initially terrified about the prospect, really, but I told Him I would open my mouth if He would put the words in me and He does exactly that. When and where He directs me in this is up to God, but I will answer when called from now on. It is the price of my freedom, and it is one that I'll gladly pay. Amen!

Chapter SIXTEEN

But seek first his kingdom and his righteousness,
and all these things will be given to you as well.
Matthew 6:33

Two Years Later

6:33 & THUNDER ON THE MOUNTAIN

For a while, I had to put this writing aside because more work was needed with my counselor, and my focus was there. I get a lot of help through my men's prayer group at church, which we call simply 6:33. It is named for the verse above. Our yearly men's retreat called men's advance was held at the YMCA Camp in Estes Park, Colorado. I have been lifted on that mountain as well as in our weekly meetings, and that is the meaning of this chapter's title. I want to honor this group and the prayer warriors who led us. These men of God have helped me to understand that if the past can help us do anything at all, it is in building a positive future for ourselves and for others. If we don't use it to do that, dwelling on it has no value anywhere. We get nothing out of replaying the past and just reliving it in our minds. We get a lot out of using our experiences to help others. Not every negative thing we experienced in the past can or has to be used to help others. Sometimes, the lesson is just for us.

– A New Counselor –

A day arrived when my counselor would gently suggest that I meet a friend of hers, a guy who also worked with people like me. At the start of my process, I could not even think of talking to another male about my struggle. She said I needed to do this in order to learn trust of males. I knew she was right, but part of me triggered at the idea. Still, I trusted her, so decided I would try to trust him as well; plus, I remembered my promise to cooperate.

When we first met, I liked him immediately. His approach was different, and he uses one that connects you to events in a safe way with the Holy Spirit leading it. Together, we would walk through more of the times they got me, then through the sadness we found there, and eventually out of that in the end. I would learn what was behind my dislike of having my picture taken. That was huge because I knew the source of my anxiety now and knew that I would someday take back my image. That would be yet another step for the future, but my work with him was a good start.

He would also walk me through my fear of a childhood toy, plastic race car tracks. I could not even hold them without shaking or being afraid inside because the predators had hit me with them. Just seeing them in the store would make me sad, too. My own toy had become a source of pain, but that too, is no longer true in me. Another thing this awesome man did for me was to help me reconnect with my family and see them in a new light. Our sessions were never easy, but like everything else, they were necessary in order for me to keep growing.

Today, I am still friends with my last counselor and the ladies who helped me, and I'm pretty sure all of us will work together in the future. We are much more then counselor and client now, we are unified in Christ as brothers and sisters. I will always love them for what they have done for me in teaching me about the love of the Father and rescuing me. They put me on a new path where I would find a home I didn't even know I had.

– Moving Forward –

Today, I am determined to try to honor God in whatever way He leads me to do so, and lead me He has. I am not always good at following His direction, but I am learning and am a work in progress. I am finally growing up inside and in Him now. That's called sanctification.

It's funny, in recent years, I felt like I had lost so many of my friends after the layoff, but today, I have amazing new friends, and mentors too. I have never really had a mentor before, and now I have more than I can count, it seems. They accept me and love me for who I am. Because I have testified before the group, they help me to move forward in healing, as I still face challenges. Even so, I have peace inside. I miss some of my old friends a lot, but they have chosen to separate themselves from me for whatever reason, so I am not looking back.

Another great thing is that my church encourages us to be members of small groups, and these groups are really a blessing. Besides the men's fellowship, I was also in a Christian writer's group and have joined a team of what my church calls "prayer warriors." As the Bible says, iron sharpens iron!

–A New Season –

I used to regularly attend two churches, but that season has come to an end. At first, I thought it was weird to have my feet in two churches, but both of my pastors told me to put my feet in a hundred churches if I wanted to. Having visited several more congregations in connecting with people, I definitely feel like an honorary member at those churches as well. Having full membership in two has led to some difficulties. I don't feel like I'm able to serve equally as well in both, so I have decided to simply become a full-time member of my new church. It is nondenominational and charismatic. That fits the new me very well. My church is Holy Spirit driven, and it is high energy like me. I feel totally at home there. The pace is not for everyone, and that is OK too. I still plan to visit my former home church as I have some awesome friends there, but we live in seasons, and this change is part of a new season for me. It's a good thing, too, and it doesn't mean I have to lose touch with those I love at my old church. We are all part of the Body of Christ.

The first time I went to the charismatic church, the senior pastor talked about a message on a poster he once saw as a young man just starting his ministry. He told us the poster had this simple message:

Jesus says, you love me as much as you love those you love the least.

It was at the start of his message, and I don't remember the rest of what he preached that night. That poster message had me wrapped around the axle big time. I could not make sense of the idea. It hit me in the gut *hard*. Those who I loved the least were those who had abused me, or so I thought. I'm not sure I yet had much love for myself either. I thought about those men; I didn't even know the names of the predators or really how many of them there could have been. The idea of loving them just totally confused me in that moment, even after all of my work in counseling. I somehow had decided that I needed to know their names before I could *really* forgive them or it somehow didn't count. How could I do that not knowing who they were, except for the one?

In a daze, I wandered into the visitor's center after the service to talk to someone to see if they could help me sort that out. I first met the associate pastor and was trying to tell him about this confusion in my mind when in walked the senior pastor, the one who had given the message. Both of these men were and are amazing. Both are my good friends today as well, along with being mentors.

That night, however, I didn't know them, and they had no idea who I was either. I can't speak for them, but I can tell you my world was about to change again. When the senior pastor walked in, the old me would normally have said yikes and gotten out of there quickly, assuming that anyone good or decent like these men could see right away what I was, or what I *believed* I was. My former mind would have screamed to run and never go back, and in the old days, I would have. I didn't run that night because the new me recognized the pardon being offered through these men of God and also the love they offered to a total stranger.

As people have learned to read my eyes, perhaps I was picking up that skill as well. I could tell immediately that even though they did not know me from Adam, they had compassion for me. I could see it clearly in their eyes. So I stumbled through trying to explain to both of them about my confusion over the poster's warning. It didn't help that I had tears in my eyes again. I finally just asked the senior pastor if he really believed what he had preached, that we could forgive anyone. Before he could give much of a reply, I said, *"What do I do if I don't know who hurt me? What if I don't know their names?"*

Even though I had started the conversation with asking if he really believed the things he preached, which is not exactly the best opening line for meeting a new pastor, he looked at me in love and just said, *"Brother, I don't know what you mean. Can you give us more?"*

The eyes looking back at me in that moment were the eyes of Jesus, and I was able to open up about my story. I told them about my abuse, and about being traded around by people. I told them that I don't see their faces in my memories, just what they did. I told them that I had tried forgiving these men, but I did not know if love is the same thing as forgiveness. I really wanted to be loving, if only I could figure out how to do it. There, it was finally out.

Connecting those two ideas was totally beyond my understanding. In answer to my question, the senior pastor gave me four powerful words. In that moment, those simple words radically changed my night and my life. They provided the answer to my struggle inside with not knowing who these strangers were. He simply said:

"It's OK; God does."

To some people, that may not sound like much of a powerful answer, but it was for me. It was exactly what I needed to hear. I understood those words immediately not just in my mind but in my heart as well. I do not have to know who those men were; I only have to want to follow God's direction. God knows our heart and fills in the details since He really does know everything. I had lived a life mostly defined by the enemy, and that simple answer broke off me one more of the enemy's chains. Today, I understand that the Holy Spirit knew exactly the words I needed to hear, and a total stranger delivered them in love and kindness to me. They would become my pastors, and also my friends after that night. You could even say we are drinking buddies today because we share the same communion table, and I have found a home.

As for loving those bad people from my past, I know now that we learn to love the person God *intended* them to be, not who they became because of sin. I certainly do not have to love what they did to me and who knows how many other boys. However, if they repent, confess to God and ask His forgiveness, God in His mercy will give it. His mercy is new every day, as scripture says, even for them. So forgive and love because Jesus does the same for us daily. God is also not asking me to accept the hurt as mine to bear; He is only asking me to love the image of them that He and wanted. He is asking that I also love the image of *me* He created and intended.

All that matters is that I am willing and wanting to love. I know something else, too. Their repentance does not let them off the hook, and there may or may not be consequences. But that is not up to me to decide, it is up to God. If they don't repent, He will deal with that and God's judgment will be more severe than anything I could think up anyway. It is His will, not mine.

So it was I went home that evening no longer confused by the poster's message. I had stepped into a new level of understanding about love and forgiveness. On the way home, I had to pull over as I was tearing up again. Along a quiet road in the darkness I stopped the car, looked up into the night sky and simply said, *"Whoever you are, I release you."*

I meant it then and I still do. It was yet another beginning of something new inside for me. I truly believe those men were probably abused as well, and part of me genuinely hurts inside for them because of that. That must sound odd. I know it would totally sound odd to the old me. My saying that doesn't excuse what they did, but releasing them released me too. I am not even sure how to describe what happened except to say that it felt like another heaviness had lifted from me. A weight I did not rightfully need to ever carry would join all of the other lies of the enemy, as it fell into a pile at my feet. That is where I left it, in the dust. With that finished, I sat there and looked up at the stars once more on a night that was clear and calm. In the shank of a quiet September evening the Lion roared in triumph as I drove away from that dark roadside toward home.

This feeling is part of the freedom Jesus promised us. He has forgiven me for all of the sins in my own life. Now I can learn to love as He does, knowing within myself that those men were not created to be predators. My prayer is that if they are still alive, they will come to know Him too and also know somehow that I have forgiven them. Christ already paid the debt in full on the cross 2,000 years ago. As my pastor would say later in another message, our forgiveness may be the best chance others have at redemption because it starts a chain reaction in the spiritual world. Through it, a harvest of righteousness comes that much closer to *their* lives, because I have *cancelled* their debt toward me. What I get in return for doing that is the same thing from Jesus, a clean slate. Scripture provides the proof of God's plan again in Micah 7:18–19, saying:

Who is a God like you, who pardons sin and forgives the transgression of the remnant of his inheritance? You do not stay angry forever but delight to show mercy. You will again have compassion on us; you will tread our sins underfoot and hurl all our iniquities into the depths of the sea.

God delights in showing mercy, and expects us to do the same. You may be saying *I don't feel like forgiving them!* I know that feeling well, all too well, in fact. For my part, I recognize that those men do not even *know* I have forgiven them. It doesn't matter; God knows, and on the cross, Jesus set the example for us. He forgave those who were at that very moment of his crucifixion going out of their way to torment Him in ways I cannot even imagine. What I suffered is nothing like what Christ suffered on the cross. Not even remotely close. God is not asking you to feel like it, He is asking you to try. When I did that, I found more peace inside. Choices lead and feelings follow! That is what I learned from a poster's message, and that's what I learned from my pastor's words too.

– A New Understanding –

My new community of fellowship has gotten me to push more deeply into the Word of God and to rediscover the Bible. My learning of its meaning today is with new eyes and a new heart for wanting to find out more. With reading the Bible, it's almost as if God has given me a do-over in learning scripture, and I'll take that gladly. Through it, we can all discover things we never knew before about God and about ourselves as well. It is an exciting book to my new eyes, and I find myself wanting to press in more closely to see everything that is in there for me. One time during Bible study while visiting a church in Louisiana, I remember thinking wow, it's like this was written just for me. I told the group that and they joyously said, *"That's right; it was!"*

Reading scripture leads us to a deeper understanding of not only who we are but *whose* we are as well. We are God's children, and no matter what sort of evil comes our way, we can run boldly into His throne room for help and just to talk. It is a learning experience, and truly everyone is a work in progress. Today, if the enemy tricks me, and yes it can still happen, I know where to turn, and I will never be fully deceived by evil again. Every time I open the Bible now, it is like opening it for the first time, with new insights. That's pretty amazing!

Chapter SEVENTEEN

The world will not be destroyed by those who do evil, but by those who watch them without doing anything.

Albert Einstein

CONVERSATIONS WITH THE SPIRIT

Today, my life is led by purpose and not desperation. It is led by the Holy Spirit, and I am no longer searching to understand what my role is or who I am. He leads me either directly through conversations with Him in prayer or by leading me to solid Christians who guide my growth in faith.

My purpose today is to write and speak about this to any and all who are willing to hear my testimony. I will not stand silently anymore. I can't do that. God rescued me and I have to share that new light He has given me. There are many others who are still trapped in that cycle of shame, guilt and fear where I spent many years. The Holy Spirit can help you just as He helped me.

I continue to learn more about love and forgiveness, lessons which began with my counselor. Then I was led to that poster's message, and that in turn is bolstered by the many people who support me now. Today, I speak those words about forgiveness and release over others and myself. I happily attended church services, no longer feeling like the best I can do is sit unnoticed on the edge and observe, hoping that something good rubs off onto me. It does. I am full on the inside now, participating and sharing what I can. I get so much from being with the people there, learning new things, but also having more fun than ever before. Church is fun now, and that is a bonus I did not expect but certainly is one I love.

Here's an example. One day, the senior pastor challenged us to give a shout-out to the Lord. I'm talking about a full-volume blast of praise to God in a shout to Him. Well, I had *never* done that before, shouted in church, so my mind said this was going to be different. Growing up, I had learned to be silent and still in church or I'd be in trouble. That night, I was not even sure I could shout, but I was sure willing to try! My first attempt, quite honestly, was kind of wimpy at best, like a mouse squeaking. Another pastor there (and friend now) was sitting beside me and smiled, saying something like, *"Really? That's the best you can do?"*

Well yes, thank you very much, were my thoughts as I grinned back at him. Actually, he wasn't being rude in that moment. He was right, it was not good enough, not by a long shot, but it was my best. I guess the senior pastor was not impressed with the group attempt either, so he called for another try from the congregation, doing so in his Louisiana style that I have come to love every week. It was then that something rose up in me and I gave a really good full-on shout-out, louder than I could have imagined. It was a yell of praise for Jesus! In that moment, I became the mouse that roared, and this time in a room full of people who were praising right along with me. What an amazing feeling it produced in me, and my other pastor friend was satisfied this time as he smiled. That feeling sticks with me to this day and now, without hesitation, I have shouted praises many times. No one looks at me funny or gets angry. They celebrate with me and why not? We all have a lot to celebrate.

I have not only learned how to shout to the Lord but also to sing loudly (if not well), raise my arms up to God's presence, hug strangers and smile for real. Best of all, I have learned to dance with abandon. My energy during praise band is like a teenager. (Scripture does promise that God will restore double what was taken from us.) Simply put, I worship like a crazy kid and dance like a bag of squirrels, not worried about what others may think because I know they dance with me in spirit if not for real. Many have told me so. My dance is to celebrate this freedom and an amazing love that is just a gift, not something I could ever earn. But I don't have to earn it because of grace. So in that, I dance because I no longer have to wear a mask or pretend to feel happiness. My happiness is real. My dance is real. Every step or hop and every shout of praise brings me closer to God. I have discovered the true joy in just being able to say thank you, Jesus!

– Rebuilding an Old Friendship –

Way back when I started this, it all began with a conversation between the Holy Spirit and myself. Actually, I was kind of rude and defensive back then. The Spirit of course knew why, and He responded with love instead of condemnation. Throughout this process, I have learned to talk to Him and to try to listen to Him as well.

It cracks me up, really, to hear some Christians say that the Holy Spirit only speaks to us on rare occasions, just once in a while, only sometimes, blah, blah, blah. Really? Where does it say that in scripture? His voice and guidance (just like His gifts) are promised to us every day, not just once in a while. I do not believe the gifts of the Holy Spirit (or being able to hear His voice) were meant only for the times of the apostles. Nothing in scripture tells me that, at least not that I have found. Scripture tells me otherwise. My friends say I hear Him because I have the faith of a child. That's amazing in itself as my childhood was stolen, but it was restored because of the work on the cross. Once saved, we are connected directly to the Spirit in ways we did not have before, and He helps us to develop our listening skills. The Spirit will speak to us daily. He does with me. Sometimes it's a message of encouragement, and sometimes it's more like spiritual parenting such as, *"OK, son, is that how we behave?"*

Such messages come to me at times when I am not acting like this new me, and they don't come in anger like the ones I heard so often growing up. When I hear the Spirit's voice in correction or affirmation, it's always given in love.

– No Fear: Tell Them –

It was during one of my conversations with the Holy Spirit that He presented me with a question. In the spring of 2014, this thought came to me from Him:

"Over 500 people have heard you speak and tell your story, yet your family does not know. What is wrong with this picture?"

I knew full well where this conversation was going and replied:

"To them, it's personal, and I don't want to hurt them with this."

His response was, as always, delivered in pure love:

"To me, it's personal, too."

I wept at that reply.

It had hurt me, it had hurt God and now it would hurt my family. I did not want to tell them because I could see no benefit in doing that, either for them or for me. In fact, I was firmly committed to *not* saying anything. I had reasoned that putting this hurt into their lives made no sense. Yet here was the Spirit saying I needed to do so for reasons I did not understand. Since this direction came from Him, I would do it, not knowing how or when or even what words to use, but that was His direction and I would follow it.

As much as I did not look forward to this I just figured He would present the time and give me the words, which He had on every single occasion. I would first tell my second oldest sister, an amazing servant of God already. She heard me out and offered nothing but love in response to this sadness. I would need her prayers to approach the rest of my family, and I had them. I would subsequently tell my other siblings and a former brother-in-law who still means a lot to me as a friend, then on to other family members. They all reacted the same, with total support and love. As I expected, it wasn't easy, but knowing the Spirit led me made it something I could do, and I'm now glad I did.

The fear that had built up inside me from years of wondering what they would think was erased and gone. The Spirit had given me the right words, and He made my siblings receptive to hearing them. I have their support now and the support of others in my family. Sometimes, survivors receive indifference or rejection when they speak, so tell or not tell is the survivor's choice. I also know that even if my family had rejected this, the Spirit would have given me the strength to walk through that too.

As it is, I am blessed to have people in my life who listen, love and don't judge me. I have their support to move forward into wherever this leads me. Of course the Spirit knew the outcome of all of this, including every step along the way. What I learned (or was reminded of once again) from this is to trust Him, surrender to Him, and go where He leads me. I had promised to do so, and He promised to be there with me through what may come. I am not always as good at listening to the Holy Spirit as I was on this issue, but like everyone else, I am a work in progress. Progress means you make mistakes and you have successes. It doesn't mean we have a flawless walk with God, only one that we are *safe* with Him no matter where the path leads.

Other conversations with the Spirit I've covered elsewhere in this book, but to me, it's amazing just to be able to talk to Him. It's like I am his only child, yet He will do the same for every human being. Try it out, tell Him you want to talk, and I *guarantee* He will listen. He's already listening, praise Jesus.

One final note on this; people have asked me, *"What does He sound like?"*

He sounds like me, but I discovered that so does the enemy, who whispers at me as well. At first this worried me as I puzzled over how I could be sure to know the difference between the two voices. You would think it is obvious, and often it is. However, the enemy is clever, and for someone new at this, it's easy to get mixed up. He'll twist scripture ever so slightly and try to trick you. A solid Christian friend gave me the answer of how to clearly tell the difference with a mnemonic as a way to remember that works perfectly for us males. He said, *"Think GAS."*

It's humorous, and OK, it appeals to guys, but here is what it stands for. GAS = glorifies God, advances the kingdom, and is scripture based. So I test every message now if I have questions. Any message from the Spirit passes all three tests and goes on to produce fruits of the Spirit as well, as described in scripture in Galatians 5:22:

But the fruit of the Spirit is love, joy, peace, forbearance, kindness, goodness, faithfulness, gentleness and self-control. Against such things there is no law. (NIV Student Bible)

Test the voices you hear with GAS. If it's the Spirit's direction, it'll pass all three and produce the fruits of the Spirit. God is not offended by your testing, either, as it shows you are listening to Him, and it should get you to press into the Bible for verification. That brings you even closer to God. It's a total a win–win thing.

I'll give you an example of how it has worked for me. When the Spirit pressed me to testify, the idea scared me a ton. I was not used to speaking about this, but here is how that message from Him passed the GAS test.

G: <u>Glorifies God</u>: Telling my story *does* glorify God, as it shows how he rescued and redeemed me, how He changed my life. It shows how He led me home, to a home I didn't know I had.

A: <u>Advances the Kingdom</u>: This one is easy. Every time I have spoken, people have come to me afterward and said it helped them. *Today, I know of around 330 people who have had their life changed by hearing me speak.* Just know that the glory and credit here go totally to Him. I am happy to be the messenger, but it's His message, not mine, and through it, lives are changed for eternity.

S: <u>Scripture Based</u>: God says in His word that He will take what is meant for our harm and turn it to good. My life is changed, and so are the lives of others. From tremendous pain comes tremendous joy now when I hear others find a closer relationship with God through my story. It doesn't shame me now. My story is God's glory, and I'll keep on speaking until He calls me home.

The stories of changed lives are the fruits of the Spirit, as one by one, people find their way to Him. Each one is a victory for God and a defeat for the enemy. It doesn't get any better than that for me.

Chapter EIGHTEEN

It is God's job to judge and the Holy Spirit's job
to convict. My job is to love.

Billy Graham

MY SOUL TO KEEP!

It has taken me a little over five years to write this, my story and my testimony. At times, I had to step back from it because I did not have any more words in that moment. Knowing the story was not yet finished, I set it aside. It is still not finished. Our freedom in Christ happens in an instant, but our growth in Him is a lifelong thing. Healing takes time and I've had to walk through some more things before this story could make sense in this, my final chapter. I am healing now and not walking alone anymore. I never really was walking alone, but at the time I didn't know it.

Reverend Graham's quote above makes me smile. It's like my story in one quote. I learned that it's God's job to judge and not mine. The Holy Spirit has done, and is still doing, a lot of conviction (or loving correction) in me. My job now? It is to love others as a reflection of the One who rescued me.

The question now is how do I bring this to a conclusion? My journey started in terror and is now rooted in freedom. It has reached a place where I can say it is finished, for now. It seems fitting for me to write a few thank you notes at this point. These are snippets of things that, while each very important to me, did not seem to fit well elsewhere in my narrative. I should say thank you once again to Jesus, and thank Him every day for the rest of my life. I also need to say thank you to all who have helped me reach this new peace inside. I am bound to miss some people, so I ask their forgiveness.

– Thank You Notes from the Fire –

1. Thank you, Jesus, for giving me back my voice. Before counseling, I could not say the *one* word that held me down in sadness like an anchor—molested. I do not fear that word anymore. To date, I have now testified and shared my story with over 6,000 people. I will keep on speaking where and when I am called to do so. This is just the beginning. Thank you, Jesus!

2. Thank you, Jesus, for giving me back my image. Christ gave me back my image. At least once, I had pornographic pictures taken of me. From that point on, I did not like having my picture taken. Today, my image of myself is no longer tied to evil memories. During the winter of 2015 my church called and asked if I would do a video testimony for Easter. My answer was an immediate yes, because of everything they had done for me. The media center pastor and I talked for about fifteen minutes. I sat there in the lights while the cameras rolled, totally comfortable in that moment.

Walking out, I stopped, frozen in my tracks in the parking lot as I realized I had just sat in front of three cameras and did not trigger once, even with talking about this. About two months before that day, the Spirit told me it was time to take back my image. I just accepted He would bring that to pass. What's amazing is that God walked me through it, and I did not even know that was happening until I was done. I don't dread having my picture taken anymore.

The video showed on Easter and went out on a live stream over the Internet to people all over the world. My church tells me that on that Easter weekend, some 282 people signed the Lamb's Book of Life and came home because of my testimony. The Spirit alone gets the credit, because in me there was never the strength to speak before. Being able to testify *on camera* and seeing the effects afterward showed me once again that God always keeps His word, always. He took something evil and turned it into something good. I have my image back. Thank you, Jesus!

3. Thank you, Jesus, for my baptism. I was baptized as a baby, but I don't remember that. I also know that I was baptized by the Spirit, and that happened on the day of my deliverance. But I'd never had the full-dunk, totally immersed in water experience. It occurred to me that Jesus was baptized as an adult in the river Jordan. Did he need to be? No, of course not, but he made a public demonstration as a way to say "This is what I expect of my believers." Jesus says if we *do not acknowledge him publicly*, he will not acknowledge us before God. I did not want to risk going there.

On the night I was baptized, I stepped out into a room of some 500 people looking on. I was energized, charged up in the Holy Spirit, and ready to go. With that, I submerged and returned to the surface to stand up soaked and clean, baptized in the name of the Father, the Son, and the Holy Spirit. I raised my hands to God in gratitude again and smiled. He smiled back at me. Thank you, Jesus!

4. Thank you, Jesus, for my mentors; as your word says, iron sharpens iron. I never really had a mentor before, but I have many now. They guide me and help me stay strong as my own understanding grows. Sometimes their words are prophetic, and sometimes they just speak encouragement over me in real love, the love of Christ. My mentors are pastors and congregation members of all ages and both genders. They know about my past and don't judge me by it. I don't sit outside anymore. Thank you, Jesus!

5. Thank you, Jesus, for showing me how I can serve others. To some people, the idea of serving others is demeaning. When I get the chance, I remember the times I have sat outside of churches listening to the music, feeling like I had no right to go into God's house. I am inside now. When I'm asked to serve, it shows me people there love me enough to ask me but totally comfortable in that moment,—yes, *me*—to do something for Christ. They trust me and believe in me. So I serve at retreats with set-up and take-down of equipment, I have gone on mission trips, I've helped bake cookies for Christmas in the church kitchen, and I will continue to say yes when I am asked. I get more out of this than I give, but it seems everyone says that. That's a good thing, as it's a double blessing from the Lord. Thank you, Jesus!

6. Thank you, Jesus, for teaching me how to reach out the way You did for me. A family once called the church because someone in their family had been caught with child pornography on his computer. One of the pastors asked if I would meet with him. I had this feeling inside like this was something I needed to do even though I didn't know why. I went to his apartment with the pastor as he was under house arrest. I told him my story that first day. Not a lot of details, but enough of them to be clear that this stuff leaves a mark. It was not meant to be hurtful. I also told him that my story is not is a sad one, but is one of victory, and that what happened to me is not the end of my story. His situation doesn't have to be the end of his story, either. After that, for over a year, I kept on communicating with him regularly. We listened to each other, and I discovered he's a man whose own past was filled with hurt as well. We shared that history in a common sadness. I came to see him not as the person in a mug shot but as someone who was reaching out to Jesus for help. Our time ended when it seemed like I had done what I could and more things started coming up for me to work on as well. I believe he is a changed man because of our time together, just as I am also changed. He is redeemed as I was. Jesus will be with him regardless of where his life leads.

Once, I met another man who had been in prison for a child pornography conviction. In his ten years there, he found Jesus, but he stood before me in tears, asking for my forgiveness. I started to tear up as well, and said, *"As one who was on the other side of that camera lens, I release you and I forgive you."*

I know he did not see the images taken of me, but I have an obligation to offer forgiveness as Christ has forgiven me for so much. I cannot withhold it from others. There is nobility in us when we do that, but it's only there because the Spirit has touched our lives. So I forgive, it's that simple to me. Thank you, Jesus!

If I ever write a second edition to this book, I'm sure there will be more thank you notes to add. They are good reminders for me, and further illustrate the ways that God has worked in my life. Maybe I'll start a new journal, one with just thank you notes to Jesus.

What do you think? For me, this is not the end, it is the beginning. Christ paved the way for me to have a real and righteous connection with God. I hope that you have walked this far with me and are starting your own journey with Him now, too. He gave me the gift of writing as a way to speak when I was in counseling and had no other way to say the words. When I started this, I didn't want any words or the reality of my past coming to the surface. Christ knew the struggle ahead and gave me what I needed to take this journey. My journal may now help others do the same, and that is my hope.

I would not wish my past on anyone, but today I would not wish it off of myself either because I can see how my life can have a meaningful impact. That lifts me, knowing that everything done for (and in me) is because God loves me more than I ever really knew. He can rescue you from whatever it is that's a struggle in your life.

This book began with the words of Jesus from John 8:32, words that I did not fully understand for a long time:

You shall know the truth, and the truth shall set you free.

I understand them now, clearly. Father, you showed me what perfect love is. You rescued me! Today, I can stand and sing and dance with real joy in your presence. As the song says, I am no longer a slave to fear. The shadows are gone from me and the great sadness has dissolved away now into nothing. I *am* loved, and I *am* finally fully and forever…free. The Lamb wins!

Amen

A Prayer for Us

Lord, I pray that we will remember you are a light amid the darkness. Jesus, thank you for enduring the road to the cross and defeating the darkness of sin that overshadowed any hope for us. Let your Holy Spirit lead us and press us to engage your Word, Lord. that it may always come alive in our hearts and be clear in our minds. Your word is a lamp for our feet and a light on our path. Let your kingdom be what wakes us up, what walks us through the day, and what lays us down at night. In the name of Jesus, the name that is above all names. Amen!

CPSIA information can be obtained
at www.ICGtesting.com
Printed in the USA
LVOW08s0901230517
535498LV00002B/346/P